OBJECT LESSONS

A book series about the hidden lives of ordinary things.

Series Editors:

Ian Bogost and Christopher Schaberg

Advisory Board:

Sara Ahmed, Jane Bennett, Johanna Drucker, Raiford Guins, Graham Harman, renée hoogland, Pam Houston, Eileen Joy, Douglas Kahn, Daniel Miller, Esther Milne, Timothy Morton, Nigel Thrift, Kathleen Stewart, Rob Walker, Michele White.

In association with

BOOKS IN THE SERIES

golf ball

HARRY BROWN

Bloomsbury Academic
An imprint of Bloomsbury Publishing Inc

B L O O M S B U R Y
NEW YORK · LONDON · NEW DELHI · SYDNEY

Bloomsbury Academic
An imprint of Bloomsbury Publishing Inc

1385 Broadway
New York
NY 10018
USA

50 Bedford Square
London
WC1B 3DP
UK

www.bloomsbury.com

**BLOOMSBURY and the Diana logo are trademarks
of Bloomsbury Publishing Plc**

First published 2015

Library of Congress Cataloging-in-Publication Data
Brown, Harry J. (Harry John), 1972-
Golf ball/Harry Brown.
pages cm
Summary: "Golf balls embody the complex human relation to the natural
world, a will to control nature, but the action of balls in play reveals the
futility of the endeavor"– Provided by publisher.
Includes bibliographical references and index.
ISBN 978-1-62892-138-0 (paperback) – ISBN 978-1-62892-139-7 (hardback)
1. Golf balls–History. I. Title.
GV976.B76 2015
796.352–dc23
2014031367

ISBN: PB: 978-1-6289-2138-0
ePDF: 978-1-6289-2141-0
ePub: 978-1-6289-2140-3

Series: Object Lessons

Typeset by Deanta Global Publishing Services, Chennai, India
Printed and bound in the United States of America

For my dad and my brother

CONTENTS

ACKNOWLEDGMENTS

With gratitude to Ian Bogost, Chris Schaberg, Haaris Naqvi, Mary Al-Sayed, and Bloomsbury for their editorial insight and support; to Michael Sinowitz for convening the reading group that introduced me to object-oriented ontology; to Anne Harris for directing me to Object Lessons; to Chris Brown for Old Head; and to Harry Brown for helping me to find true gravity.

PART ONE

OUT: THING

1 HOW I CUT A GOLF BALL IN HALF, AND FOUND A LOT OF THINGS INSIDE

In Jamie Uys's 1980 film *The Gods Must Be Crazy*, Xi, a Bushman living an isolated and peaceful life in the Kalahari Desert, chances upon a Coca-Cola bottle dropped in the sand. The bottle is litter from an airplane passing overhead, but Xi has never seen a glass bottle, an airplane, or any other artifact of the modern world. He decides that the glistening object is a gift from the gods and takes it to his clan. Like Xi, they have never seen anything with such clarity and hardness and find it "the strangest and most beautiful thing they had ever seen." Their fascination with "the thing" soon turns to jealously. People fight for its possession and finally use it as a weapon knocking each other on the head. Confused that the gods sent something to make them unhappy, the people now judge it an "evil thing." Xi decides to take it to the end of the world, where he will throw it back to the gods. "The thing," he says, "does not belong on the earth."[1]

Around the same time that Uys made this memorable film, I was an 8-year-old boy living an isolated and peaceful life in rural Pennsylvania, and one day I chanced upon a large bucket of golf balls dropped in the street. A neighbor had cleaned his garage and left the old balls—scuffed, scarred, and discarded—at the end of his driveway with some other trash, awaiting the garbage truck. I scavenged the balls and took them to my friends. None of us played golf, so it remained for us to discover a purpose for this unexpected windfall. We found that they were dense, like super balls, and though they had hard shells, they bounced and danced and shot with astounding liveliness when rolled or slammed on the pavement. We sent them through drainage pipes, cast them into the creek, and tried to whack them with baseball bats. We had no golf clubs. We lived in the age before Tiger Woods, and golf was still a game for old men in country clubs. We pegged each other with them, like the Bushmen with their bottle, but they hurt. We stopped weaponizing them, wary of our mutually assured destruction, and soon got bored. I set them on a dusty shelf in the basement and forgot about them.

Some time later, on a slow day, I was rooting listlessly in the basement, looking for some diversion among the tools and old toys. I found the golf balls and recalled their uncompromising hardness, their surprising jumpiness. What gave them this weird life? What was inside? I took one of the balls and put it in a vise. I turned the crank and increased the pressure. I expected it to pop like a blister or crack like a walnut, but it had great pliability for its apparent hardness. It compressed like a tennis ball, seeming to defy my efforts to break it open. Its unexpected resistance alarmed me. As I turned the crank, I thought it might slip the grip of the vise, pop out, and shoot with all of its elastic force right into the center of my forehead.

I relaxed the crank and reversed the pressure, still holding the ball in the vise. Then I found a hacksaw and started to cut it in half from the top down. As I sliced through the white shell, I sensed its internal force being released in something like a controlled explosion. A bundle of tightly wound rubber twine beneath the shell began to snap and unwind as the saw penetrated more deeply. At last, I hit the core: a gray rubber shell in the center of the coiled bands popped and spewed an acrid liquid in my face. I killed the thing, but not before it spit its dying insult.

I completed the bisection, removed the two halves from the vise, and examined them. I thought of the pictures in my science book showing a cross section of the Earth, with its thin, hard crust, its squishy mantle, and its volatile, mysterious core. It seemed like a tiny planet, with hidden layers concealing an internal pressure, a compressed energy. Inside, I found not only its rubber and liquid innards but also something less tangible. What gave me the feeling that I'd discovered in this mundane, discarded object an inner life?

Probing the gap between things and the ways we experience them, Heidegger suggested that we only really know an object when it breaks—not because physical rupture provides a glimpse of internal structure, but rather because a loss of function liberates it from its relation to us. We cannot know a hammer, for instance, except through its uses as a tool for banging nails in the workshop or bashing skulls on the battlefield. When the hammer breaks and suddenly loses this usefulness, it appears to us as it really is, apart from its relation to us.

Heidegger's insight provides a clue about the uncanny sense of discovery I experienced when I broke the golf ball. My bisection not only severed one hemisphere from the other but also severed the object from its use. At the moment it split in the vise, it ceased to be—and became—a golf ball, losing its purpose as something to smack with a club but emerging in fullness as something else, with its layers of rubber twine and its liquid heart: a planet in miniature. Discovering the golf ball in this way gave me a strangely lucid apprehension of the object. As Xi finds the bottle—which, for him, is not a "bottle" for storing and drinking Coke but a "thing" of unknown origin and purpose—I found the golf ball on its own terms and detected in its guts encoded information about how we make things, how we use things, and how we throw things away.

Annals of the game record that the earliest golf balls were made of wood. Next came the "featherie," a stitched leather pouch stuffed with moistened chicken or goose feathers, stitched shut, and dried into a hard, tight spheroid. In the nineteenth century, the "guttie," a handful of gutta-percha latex molded into a solid pill, replaced the feather ball. Much cheaper than the handcrafted featheries, the mass-produced gutties opened the game to the middle class and created a demand for more golf courses everywhere, transforming recreational landscapes throughout America and Britain. In the twentieth century, layered planetesimals with balata crusts and rubber band mantles, like the one I vivisected in my basement, came into use. Today, golf balls fly farther than ever, rendering many old courses obsolete and leading golf purists to argue for strict regulation on further advances in ball construction. Consisting of synthetic polymers practically impervious to damage or decay, they appear destined, like almost all of our plastic creations, to long outlive us. T. S. Eliot recognized the object as a capsule of modernity, musing that a future age will look back to our own time and find that we were a "decent and godless people," whose only monuments were the "asphalt road" and "a thousand lost golf balls."[2]

As we move from Heidegger's vision of a thing in itself to Eliot's vision of the universal in the particular, we discover, like Xi on his journey out of the Kalahari to the fringe of civilization, that full comprehension of the thing also means seeing it within the social and economic systems that generate it, locating it within webs of things and ideas. For Timothy Morton, objects consist as much in their complex web of relations to other objects as they do in their lonely being.

"Objects can't be exhausted by perception," he writes. "When you approach an object, more and more objects emerge."[3] Within its expansive interobjective web, the Titleist that we hold between thumb and forefinger forms only one part of the much greater but only dimly perceptible ecology of objects that includes, we will see, chickens, cows, Malaysia, bulldozers, spandex shorts, the hydrogen bomb, the Loch Ness monster, and the moon. Just as every cell in the body contains the genetic imprint and evolutionary history of the whole organism, every manufactured object contains an imprint of our civilization, a thumbnail sketch of our history, and, as Eliot imagined, perhaps even a glimpse of our senescence and eventual desolation.

When we conceive of this web of relations between things, we begin to access what seems inaccessible: the world beyond its relation to us. This revelation, finally, is the purpose of this book: to discover the essential depth and weirdness in the most banal and ubiquitous of objects, the thing that my neighbor left for the garbage truck. More particularly, I want to see what we can learn by applying an object-oriented perspective to the study of games and sports. If we shift our focus from the great players, great courses, and great tournaments that dominate many golf books to the spherical singularity at the center of it all, we can unlock hidden dimensions of the game, new insights about its history and how we play it today. In the first half of this course of chapters, I will trace the history of the golf ball and its relation to other objects and to the landscapes of the game. In the second half,

I will explore the way it shapes our consciousness of play and the natural environment, while at the same time speculating about its existence beyond our consciousness as part of the material substrate of some future archaeology that defines our age. Like Xi, I intend to pick up the thing dropped at my feet and take it to the end of the world.

2 HOW THE GOLF BALL KEEPS HOLY THE LORD'S DAY

Michael Murphy's book, *Golf in the Kingdom*, relates the imagined detour of the author, a philosophy student on his way to India to study with Sri Aurobindo, to Burningbush links in the Kingdom of Fife. Here he meets Shivas Irons, a local golf guru, and finds that he doesn't need to go to an ashram to find enlightenment. He plays a round with Shivas, glimpses what he calls the hidden structure of reality, and then joins Shivas and his friends at a convivial dinner party to drink whiskey and discuss the nature of golf. Here Shivas speaks about the mysterious Seamus MacDuff, his own golf teacher who "invented the game so long ago."[1]

MacDuff, we learn, is a kind of benevolent daemon haunting the ravine below the thirteenth hole at Burningbush, where Shivas takes Murphy for a midnight golf lesson. The two arrive at a small cave where, local legend says, Seamus makes his retreat. They find there a finely balanced shillelagh—Seamus's "baffing spoon"—and two featheries, which they hit at a rough stone target. Seamus appears only momentarily as a ghostly presence on the cliff above the ravine. The hoary spirit personifies what Murphy sees as a purifying return to the game's origins: a wild landscape, a rough wooden club, a flying wad of cowhide and chicken feathers.

In the enchanted prehistory of the game that Shivas and Murphy, in their search for Seamus, mean to recover, players batted balls hewn from boxwood or ash. Following the Peace of Glasgow between Scotland and England in 1502, when Scotsmen liberated their muster fields for leisure, royal accounts show that James IV of Scotland bought clubs and balls from a Perth bowyer, who probably made golfing equipment with the same lathe that he used to make crossbows for James's army. Continental Europeans had a long familiarity with featheries, or balls like them. The Romans used the *paganica*, a spherical leather pouch stuffed with feathers or wool, for sports resembling croquet or field hockey. These Roman diversions evolved into a variety of stick-and-ball games played throughout Europe during the Middle Ages, using stuffed balls descended from the *paganica*. James and the late medieval Scots, however, played golf to the crack of wood on wood. The story of the emergence of feather balls in Scotland—the way those two magical little sacks found their way into Seamus's cave—involves a curious triangulation of events, including the rediscovery of Roman ball-making techniques in Scotland, the ebbing of religious zeal, and the sale of royal monopolies. Ultimately, the emergence of the feather ball in the seventeenth century marks an important moment in the history of golf: the first effort to commodify the ball and nationalize the game.

Today, professional golf tournaments consist of seventy-two holes, four rounds of eighteen, played from Thursday to Sunday, with the trophies and big money won and lost on the Lord's Day. Among the most hallowed traditions in the game are the final round of the Masters on Easter Sunday and the final round of the US Open on Father's Day. We can hardly imagine a time when churchmen would forbid people to play golf on Sundays, as they did in Scotland in the late sixteenth and early seventeenth centuries. Then, as now, the Sabbath was the best day for golf—most people spent the other days working. For a whole generation, however, religious reformers guarded the sanctity of the Sabbath against golf and other profanities—such favorite Scots pastimes as loitering, drinking, dancing, archery, carrick, and shinty—withering the game.

In 1618, James VI and I, monarch of a unified Scotland and England, decided to reverse the policy. When, James asks in a royal proclamation, "shall the common people have leave to exercise, if not upon the Sundays and holidays, seeing they must apply their labor and win their living in all working days"? The king rebukes the overly "precise" churchmen and decrees that "our good people be not disturbed, letted, or discouraged from any lawful recreation," provided that they attend divine service before their fun and games.[2] In the same year that James made his proclamation, the feather golf ball made its first appearance in Scotland. Murphy calls the two events a happy "coincidence," offering only vague speculation that "every improvement of leisure got into laws and treaties, and politics generally."[3] But were the new golf ball and the new rule more directly connected? How did the transformation of the golf ball change the way Scotland and England kept holy the Lord's Day?

In *A History of Golf*, Robert Browning cites a 1618 writ of James VI and I granting the merchant James Melville a monopoly on the golf ball trade. The preamble states that the "Sovereign Lord and King understands that there is no small quantity of gold and silver transported yearly out of his Highness's kingdom of Scotland for the buying of golf balls, used in that kingdom for the recreation of his Majesty's subjects."[4] While historians sometimes cite this writ as evidence of the game's origins in the Netherlands, which exported the balls to Scotland, Browning reads the preamble as a rhetorical cloak for royal profiteering through the sale of monopolies, one of the abuses that led to the outbreak of civil war in 1642. Having purchased the monopoly from the king, Melville could then sell licenses to ball manufacturers, who in turn could pass the increased cost to individual buyers. Browning argues that some "specious and fair-seeming phrases"[5] about protecting English trade would nominally conceal the king's true motive, which was to claim a share of the profits of Melville's golf ball business. The transaction signals the genesis of golf as an economic phenomenon. As Browning concludes, "the most interesting point about the whole thing is that in 1618 the trade in golf balls was sufficiently important to make a monopoly worth securing."[6] Golf balls, in other words, had become profitable enough to be a new source of national revenue.

Browning speculates that the new economic significance of golf balls resulted from a qualitative change in the materials used to construct them. In fact, he notes a substantial rise in the cost of golf balls just prior to the writ of monopoly, suggesting that the increase in value had to do with something other than the king claiming his share of the trade. During the reign of James VI and I, the price of golf balls increased twelvefold, a hike that Browning attributes to a significant change in the "form and make" of the ball. The writ identifies William Berwick as the sole manufacturer, but why should Melville bother to secure a monopoly for the sake of a single license? If Melville and Berwick "were the first people to start manufacturing a new type of ball and wanted to keep the others out," Browning concludes, "the reference [to Melville and Berwick in the writ] has a sort of sense."[7] The monopoly, in effect, would serve as a patent on the new feather ball, mutually enriching the king as grantor, Melville as retailer, and Berwick as manufacturer. Such an arrangement could certainly induce the king to end the prohibition against playing golf on Sunday; more people playing golf on Sunday meant more people playing golf generally, and that meant more people buying the new feather golf balls.

The new balls covered by the writ were produced and sold at high expense. While any carpenter could turn a wooden ball on a lathe, making a featherie required more skill and attention. It consisted of a leather pouch sewn from three pieces of hide, stuffed with a hatful of moist feathers, and finished with white paint. Ball makers stitched the leather cover first, turned it inside out to protect the seams, and then injected the feathers into the pouch with an iron spike. As the ball dried, the leather cover contracted and the feathers inside expanded, giving the ball a surprising hardness. The whole process required several hours of labor and considerable strength to compress the feathers. In 1650, replacing a lost ball cost nearly as much as replacing a broken club. In the nineteenth century, just prior to the invention of gutta-percha balls, one featherie cost as much as five shillings, the equivalent of twenty dollars today.[8] Moreover, the softness of the materials and quirks in the crafting often yielded wobbly asymmetrical orbs that flew erratically, became soggy and sluggish in wet conditions, and could bear far less punishment than their gutta-percha and polyurethane successors.

The featherie's unfortunate combination of fragility and expense made golf balls a profitable trade for merchants like Melville and Berwick, but also made the game an exclusive pursuit, prohibiting play for anyone who could not afford to replace lost or damaged balls. The plight of the common golfer in the age of the featherie finds voice in William

Graham, a member of the Innerleven Club, who composed a lament for his lost and battered balls:

Though Gouf be of our games most rare,
Yet, truth to speak, the tear and wear
O' balls was felt to be severe,
  And source of great vexation.
When Gourlay balls cost half-a-croun,
And Allan's no' a farthing doun,
The feck o's wad been harried soon
  In this era of taxation.[9]

For all of their flaws, however, featheries represented a quantum leap in ball construction. In good conditions, good players could drive them more than 200 yards—comparable to the distances we drive golf balls today. Superior in its flight to the inert wooden ball, the feather ball set the standard for the game until the discovery of gutta-percha in the middle nineteenth century. In a larger context, the evolution of the golf ball from a wooden pellet to a wad of leather and feathers elevated its economic importance, as James integrated the golf ball trade into the royal budget and, in effect, nationalized the game. The correlation between royal profit from the new balls and the king's loosening of religious restrictions suggests that the feather golf ball, in a small way, might have fostered the process of secularization in Scotland, moving the country closer toward its Enlightenment, or at least helping to stem the zeal that curtailed the enjoyment of loiterers, drinkers, dancers, and golfers throughout the country. At the same time, the expensive new ball also set the game on the path to elitism, as duffers like poor William Graham, harried by errant shots and high taxes, could no longer afford to keep up with the game.

The initial emergence of a ball of Roman design in Scotland in the early seventeenth century remains mysterious. How did James Melville and William Berwick come to possess a new kind of golf ball prior to their purchase of the monopoly? Did some traveler, lately returned from a continental journey, tell them about the lighter, livelier balls that Italian or Dutch sportsmen used in their games? Did the traveler, indeed, return with one of these balls, inspiring Melville's entrepreneurialism? However Scots ball makers found the inspiration to abandon the lathe for leather and feathers, 1618 represents an *annus mirabilius* for golf. In this year, the ball not only became an economic force but also liberated Scots and English golfers, having dutifully attended divine service in the morning, to take up their baffing spoons in the afternoon and curse the Almighty with every hook and slice.

3 HOW AN EMPIRE MADE THE GOLF BALL, AND THE GOLF BALL MADE AN EMPIRE

In 1839, while William Graham and his mates fuffed and shied their feather balls at Innerleven, colonial expansion into Southeast Asia introduced European manufacturers to the unique properties of gutta-percha, a natural latex extracted from the family of *Palaquium* trees native to Malaysia. Gutta-percha has an important property that many latex rubbers do not. Pliable when hot, it becomes rigid, though not brittle, when cooled. As the first commercial plastic, it made an ideal substance for molding and mass-producing a variety of consumer goods, including furniture, dental fillings, jewelry, gun components, canes, toys, roof shingles, shoes, pipes, cisterns, ear-trumpets, boats, hat molds, packing material, and electrical fuses.

The most important application of gutta-percha, however, was its use as insulation in transoceanic telegraph cables, which became essential in maintaining communication between the distant corners of colonial empires. The historian John Tully describes this network of telegraph wires as the "nerves" of the British Empire, connecting the "brain" in London to the many "eyes and ears" scattered across the frontiers of six continents. Building this neural network, Tully explains, required the profligate destruction of many millions of *Palaquium* trees in Malaysian rainforests, finally leading to the collapse of the gutta-percha trade and, in the longer term, the irrevocable destruction of Southeast Asian ecosystems: a "Victorian ecological disaster."[1]

We have two curiously different narratives about the invention of the gutta-percha golf ball in 1848. In the first version, there is no inventor; rather, he is some anonymous cog in a Victorian rubber factory. Browning speculates that it might have been somebody at W. T. Henley's Telegraph Works, a company with prior experience using gutta-percha for cables.[2] In the second version, the inventor is a university student, Robert Adams Paterson, who loves golf but cannot afford to play with featheries. When Paterson, having made his career as a minister and educator, died in Rochester in 1904, a *New York Times* obituary recounted an understated but compelling story of discovery:

Dr. Paterson was born in Scotland seventy-five years ago, and when a boy attended St. Andrew's University. Golf was played there extensively, but a pigskin ball was used which was stuffed with feathers, and was very expensive.

Dr. Paterson said he was too poor to own or buy a pigskin ball, and he experimented with other materials, finally using gutta percha which had been wrapped around an idol sent from India. It worked so well that in the course of time gutta percha was exclusively used.[3]

In this cherished narrative of golf history, poverty and a passion for the game breed ingenuity. With his own bare hands, Paterson molds packing material into a new kind of ball, transforming trash into a sporting revolution. We find in these two versions of the invention of the gutta-percha ball the first instance of a recurring theme: competing claims of origin that pit a native Scots genius against a faceless factory machine. As we will see again with the invention of the wound ball, this theme illustrates an underlying tension between the increasing influence of industrial technology on golf and the pastoral traditions of the game.

Regardless of its origin, the guttie had a profound influence. It flew farther and less erratically than the featherie, particularly after the application of dimples, and it proved much more durable and resistant to moisture. It rolled straighter on the green, contributing to better putting and better scores. Most significantly, it was much cheaper, about a fifth of the cost of a feather ball. As the story of young Paterson suggests, the many golfers barred from the game by the cost of featheries embraced the guttie, and golf itself, with new enthusiasm. Makers of the old feather balls, an institution of the game for more than three centuries, suddenly saw a threat to their complacency. Browning relates the panic of John Gourlay, the maker of the "half-a-croun" balls of William Graham's lament, when he witnessed a match played with the new gutta-percha balls. At that moment, Gourlay decided to shift from manufacturing to retail, ordering six dozen gutties that he would sell to supplement what would soon be a very slow business in featheries.[4]

As Browning explains, however, tradesmen like Gourlay, when adaptable, "found the loss of revenue from ball-making far more than made up by the vast increase in the number of players taking up the game, whose chief drawback up to then had been the short life of the expensive feathery balls."[5] Browning and other golf historians commonly attribute this "golf boom," beginning in the later nineteenth century, to the guttie, an object responsible for transforming golf from an insular diversion played mostly by the gentry to a synecdoche for bourgeois leisure around the world.

The wound ball that replaced the gutta-percha ball, though different in construction, emerged from the same industrial processes that led to the invention of the guttie. The story of its invention relates the same homespun ingenuity that we find in Robert Paterson's obituary. Coburn Haskell was dawdling at the B. F. Goodrich factory in Akron, Ohio, in 1898, while waiting for his friend, factory boss Bertram Work, to meet him for a round of golf. Haskell idly picked up some rubber twine, wound it into a tight little sphere, and bounced it on the factory floor: the improvised ball jumped and rolled with astonishing life. Haskell and Work immediately collaborated on a design with a liquid core and a hard gutta-percha cover, secured a patent to produce the new balls in the factory, and in 1902 invented the "Haskell ball," the template for the thing I vivisected in my basement in 1980.

Over time, cores became larger and covers became thinner and more durable. Manufacturers experimented with a variety of substances for the core—including mercury, hair, soap, blood, ball bearings, compressed air, wood, treacle, glycerin, castor oil, tapioca, honey, pulverized metal, soil, rubber, cork, and celluloid—until they discovered that plain water worked best. Balata, a softer kind of latex extracted from South American trees, soon replaced gutta-percha as the cover material.

The first players using Haskell balls observed the same amazing jauntiness that fascinated me as a boy when I discovered the cache of balls in the street. "Its greater elasticity at first made it seem more difficult to control on the green," Browning writes, "but for ladies, for young players, and for old ones, it made golf a different game, and if its liveliness occasionally made it bound into places the gutta ball would have never reached, this was more than balanced by its readier response to the player's efforts from these and other awkward lies."[6] As Browning's description of its properties suggests, the Haskell ball, whatever its core, offered players significant improvements over the guttie: less shock to the hands, more compression, more loft, and more distance.

The layered ball conceived by Haskell established the basic design that continues to define the current market, largely dominated by two- or three-piece balls with polyurethane covers, mantles, and cores. According to the USGA Conforming Golf Balls list, a detailed compendium of all of the balls on current market approved for regulation play, about half consist of two pieces, a solid core with a single cover. About a quarter consist of three pieces, with a solid core and two covers, or a solid core and mantle with one cover. The new OnCore ball has a hollow metal core with a mantle and cover. The remaining quarter includes balls with four or five pieces consisting of some novel configuration of outer covers, inner covers, intervening mantles, outer cores, and inner cores. The Maxfli U/6 represents the first ball composed of six pieces, including a solid core, four mantle layers, and a cover.[7]

In terms of ball manufacture, we find direct continuity between the industrialization of the golf ball in the nineteenth century and the present market. Four of today's major ball manufacturers started by making tires and other rubber products before diversifying or specializing exclusively in golf balls: Acushnet (Pinnacle and Titleist balls), Bridgestone (Bridgestone, Precept, and TourStage balls), Dunlop (DDH, Maxfli, Srixon, and XXIO balls), and Yokohama (PRGR balls). These four companies combine to produce almost half of the balls on the Conforming Golf Balls list: in other words, half of the present market share in golf balls belongs to four manufactures that emerged from the colonial rubber trade.

Yet Haskell's original wound ball and those that imme- diately followed would not conform to USGA standards today. The list contains nothing with a mantle of rubber twine or a core of ball bearings, cork, or tapioca. Haskell's inspired construction, which once transformed the game, seems in the age of synthetic polymers a goofy *fin-de-siècle* contraption of popping rubber bands and a surprise center. While the design combining multiple layers with varying properties remains consistent between Haskell's day and our own, the materials and the means of producing these objects have changed radically, just as the age of colonial empires has given way to the age of space travel.

Still, the guttie and Haskell ball represent the advent of modernity in golf—in the materials and means of production of the ball, and in the socioeconomic and geographic expansion of the game. As one of many industrial by-products of the destruction of Malaysian jungles for the mass production of telegraph cables, the gutta-percha ball probably contributed little, in itself, to the "Victorian ecological disaster" that Tully describes. At the same time, the new ball started the development of golf as a transcontinental pastime, leading to the emergence of the game we know today. As a by-product of the British Empire, the gutta-percha ball was the seed for the new empire of golf.

4 HOW THE GOLF BALL BLEW UP AMERICA AND MADE GOLF MORE FUN

John Updike, who died in 2009, played golf for most of his adult life, but he wasn't having as much fun by 1990, when he wrote his essay "The Big Bad Boom." In it, he claimed that golf had lost its soul. All around, he observed, the sport was booming. Americans played about a billion rounds of golf annually and spent nearly a billion dollars on balls, bags, clubs, and carts. More people than ever, including women, minorities, and young people, had adopted the game.[1] But all this money and all these people threatened what Updike loved most about golf—the tranquil intimacy with a beautiful landscape. He laments the overcrowding and the punishment endured by fairways and greens: "The course isn't just overplayed, it's pillaged."[2] With nostalgia, he recalls the "charm of walk-along, rough-and-ready golf," rounds played with good friends, during lazy summer afternoons, on sleepy local courses unharried by the millions late to take up the game.[3] "Golf's great gift to the spirit is space," he writes, "and the space in this case was organically designed and blessedly, blissfully underpopulated." Now, he says, golf is "in a losing battle for the precious planetary surface," and the cost of building and maintaining new courses dictates that they "can only be built as carpeting between condos or as private retreats for the scarily rich."[4]

This "big bad boom," articulated by Updike as a crisis, signals an interesting moment in golf history. Somehow, the game starts to lose allure just as it reaches its zenith in both acreage and popularity. We can trace the root of the crisis to the turn of the twentieth century, when the advent of gutta-percha and wound balls spurred the demographic and geographic expansion of the game and fostered new theories of course design. What, then, does the evolution of the golf ball have to do with the evolution of the golf course—and with having fun?

Many of the quiet, out-of-the-way courses Updike remembers so fondly were, in fact, products of the boom in an earlier phase, when new courses cropped up all over the country to accommodate waves of new players, initially drawn to the game by the availability of cheaper, tougher, and livelier balls. At Spalding, Tom Bendelow, the "Johnny Appleseed" of the golf boom, believed that the best way to sell more balls and clubs was to build more courses, making golf more accessible to more people. Bendelow created cheap public courses for the new golfing masses, often constructed in existing public parks and in the midst of established communities.[5] The even more prolific Donald Ross designed or remodeled seventy-one courses between 1900 and 1917, averaging one about every three months. By the end of his career, Ross created over 400 golf courses across the country.[6] Reporting on Ross's work, a London journalist described him as "The Man Who Is Blowing up America," with his dynamite and bulldozers, to create a new national landscape where golf courses, public parks, and lawns formed the sprawling green continuum of a burgeoning suburbia.[7]

The effect on the "planetary surface," as Updike says, has been measurable. In 1894, the Amateur Golf Association, later the United States Golf Association (USGA), was formed by five founding members. By 1910 the USGA had 267 member clubs, by 1932 it had 1,138, and by 1980 it had over 5,000. Today the USGA has nearly 10,000 member clubs, though not all of the golf courses in the United States are part of the organization.[8] The National Golf Foundation estimates that there are about 15,500 courses in the country.[9] With each of these courses covering nearly 200 acres, the United States contains almost 5,000 square miles of golf land, an area the size of Connecticut. England has witnessed a similar proliferation of golf courses relative to its size. In 1850, Blackheath was the only golf club in the country; by 1880 there were twelve, and by 1887 there were fifty. More than 1,000 golf clubs dotted the English countryside by 1914, when the First World War curbed the boom and initiated a period of more modest growth. Today England has about 2,700 golf courses.[10] More than 35,000 golf courses exist worldwide, covering about 10,000 square miles, an area roughly the size of Massachusetts.[11] On a planetary scale, the transformation of farmland and wilderness to golf courses has not been immense, but neither has it been invisible.

With the discovery of more durable materials and more efficient means of production, the evolution of the golf ball has radiated outward, changing the landscapes of the game and the ways we experience them. Perhaps more interesting than the rapid proliferation of new courses during the boom, new and more articulate theories of design emerged in the process. Beautiful as they are, the earliest golf links took shape in a theoretical vacuum, formed not by architects with blueprints and bulldozers, but rather by players who trod the natural pathways from tee to green. Golfers fondly say that God, or nature, was golf's first architect—a notion that has long inspired mortal course architects to pursue the "organic design" that enchants Updike. Alister MacKenzie, for example, describes course architecture as a fine art in imitation of nature, advocating an aesthetic ideal founded on the paradoxical aesthetic of cultivated wildness. MacKenzie's "general principles," outlined in *The Spirit of St. Andrews*, emulate the features of original links courses, emphasizing the integration of artificial features indistinguishable from natural surroundings and an openness that invites players to plot their own route to the green, as if exploring a beautifully contrived garden.[12] He says that course design begins by creating artificial features that "harmonize with the natural surroundings" and urges the designer to "imitate the beauties of nature."[13] He muses that the undulations of links land are like the waves upon the sea.[14] For MacKenzie, a golf course is an exploded garden, holding our consciousness in a delicate, liminal state of pleasure between artificiality and wildness.

The aesthetic emulation of early golf courses like St. Andrews, those formed by the action of wind and water on the coastal fringes of Scotland, reflects a nostalgia among architects like MacKenzie and players like Updike for the pastoral age of the game, when its practitioners made their own balls from chicken feathers and cowhide, and courses required no greenskeepers save for rabbits to chew the fairway turf. The invention of the gutta-percha and wound golf balls shook golf from this charmed idyll by throwing the game open to masses of new players and creating unprecedented demand for new courses. In terms of course architecture, the evolution in golf ball construction led to an inversion in the fundamental relation between the game and the land. Course architects like Bendelow and Ross no longer searched for picturesque land for golf courses but rather engineered the picturesque anywhere they wanted. The fundamental task of the course architect changed from adapting golf to the landscape to adapting the landscape to golf.

Liberated by new technical capabilities to mold the earth, designers began to explore the newly discovered plasticity and ludic potential of the landscape. Following the invention of the gutta-percha ball and the subsequent boom in course construction, we witness the emergence of three predominant schools of design. The penal school employs hazards primarily to punish bad shots, and courses conceived this way often prove to be too difficult for the beginning player. The strategic school uses hazards not to penalize but rather to compel the player to consider different options for approaching the green. The arrangement of hazards makes the shortest line to the green the most risky but also offers weaker players other approaches, with less risk and less reward. As a kind of combination of the penal and strategic schools, the heroic school presents a significant advantage gained by a long carry from the tee, forcing golfers to assess their own abilities and privileging more skilled players. Golf architect Tom Doak claims that the arrangement of hazards according to these different schools of design constitutes the "essence of interesting golf," arguing that the best courses borrow concepts from all three schools. "Amen Corner" at Augusta National, perhaps the most revered of any three holes in golf, includes "one purely strategic hole" in the par-four eleventh, "one essentially penal hole" in the par-three twelfth with its famous water hazard, and a "classic heroic hole" in the short par-five thirteenth.[15]

As the architect of Amen Corner, MacKenzie adapted much of what he knew about course architecture, particularly bunker placement and design, from his experience in trench combat during the First World War, when he had to use the landscape to camouflage infantry and artillery emplacements.[16] As MacKenzie suggests, both military camouflage and course architecture involve an imitation of nature, with the artifice of design concealed. MacKenzie's attempt to create good golf using the same techniques he used to deceive and destroy German infantry in the war seems to manifest a bipolar theory of design, but his mixed attitude of sympathy and antagonism toward the player only demonstrates a mindful balancing of ease and frustration to foster a deeply satisfying navigation of landscape.

In his book, *Flow*, the psychologist Mihaly Csikszentmihalyi identifies this same elegant combination of difficulty, choice, and reward as the basic formula for producing the experience we call *fun*. In this state of heightened emotion and cognition, he explains, our intellectual and physical capabilities meet and overcome a difficult, but not impossible, challenge. "Contrary to what we usually believe, moments like these, the best moments in our lives, are not the passive, receptive, relaxing times," Csikszentmihalyi writes. "The best moments usually occur when a person's body or mind is stretched to the limits of voluntary effort to accomplish something difficult and worthwhile."[17] In his memoir, *Golf Is My Game*, Bobby Jones reveals that he and MacKenzie implemented the same philosophy in their design of Augusta National. "As far as possible," Jones writes, "there should be presented to each golfer an interesting problem which will test him without being so impossibly difficult that he will have little chance for success. There must be something to do, but that something must always be within the realm of reasonable accomplishment."[18]

Csikszentmihalyi claims that simple challenges bore the player, while insoluble ones frustrate him. Fun lives in the channel between boredom and frustration. As an individual player's skill increases, the challenge posed by the game must likewise increase."[19] At Augusta, MacKenzie and Jones solve the problem of creating challenges for players of different skill levels by offering players a choice of playable routes to the green: a heroic carry over a formidable hazard, or a safer "strategic" path around the hazard. Jones recalls that he and MacKenzie agreed on two fundamental principles: "First, there must be a way around for those unwilling to attempt the carry; and second, there must be a definite reward awaiting the man who makes it. Without the alternative route the situation is unfair. Without the reward it is meaningless."[20] He calls the thirteenth, the final hole at Amen Corner, "one of the finest holes for competitive play that I have ever seen" for the series of strategic choices with varying levels of risk and reward that it offers the player. Jones writes of his own creation:

> The player is first tempted to dare the creek on his tee shot by playing in close to the corner, because if he attains his position he has not only shortened the hole, but obtained a more level lie for his second shot. Driving out to the right not only increases the length of the second, but encounters an annoying side-hill lie.[21]

The second shot on this par-five also "entails a momentous decision whether or not to try for the green." A successful carry to the green gives the player a deserved reward: a putt for eagle. An unsuccessful attempt at this heroic carry will likely leave the ball in the creek at the front of the green, a two-stroke penalty that will almost certainly result in a bogey or worse.[22]

We still find MacKenzie and Jones's principles dramatically illustrated at Augusta. In the 2014 Masters, the thirteenth hole indeed proved to be the best scoring opportunity of the tournament, yielding more eagles and birdies than any other hole on the course. The tour professionals consistently succeeded in skirting the creek with the drive and reaching the green with the second shot, reaping the reward that remains elusive for the less "heroic," everyday players at Augusta. The eleventh hole, the first at Amen Corner, proved to be the most dangerous, forcing more bogeys and double bogeys than any other hole, often by punishing an inaccurate second shot with a water hazard to the left of the green and a bunker to the right.[23]

While Augusta represents one of the purest expressions of the aesthetic and ludic theories to emerge from the golf boom, the changes in ball construction, the subsequent proliferation of new courses, and the rising popularity of the game also contained the seeds of the malaise that Updike articulates a century later. In the quarter-century since Updike's jeremiad, however, the boom has gone bust. According to the National Golf Foundation, the game has lost five million players in the last decade and may lose twenty percent of its existing twenty-five million players in the next, as baby boomers start to die off. Young players have not filled the gap, complaining that the game is too difficult to learn, too expensive and time-consuming, and too tiresome with its complex rules and etiquette.[24] They have become disenchanted with the game not because it's too crowded, as Updike complained twenty-five years ago, but rather because it's too boring.

In response, many in the sport have begun to ask what makes golf fun in the first place and what seems to be missing. Ted Bishop, president of the Professional Golfers' Association of America (PGA), said: "We've got to offer more forms of golf for more people to try. We have to get them in the fold, and then maybe they'll have this idea it's supposed to be fun."[25] HackGolf, a website created by a golf merchandise executive to crowdsource ideas to revive the game, aims to diagnose the "fun problem" by asking simply, "How would you make golf more fun?"[26] A number of club professionals have joined Bishop in devising a new "recreational" style of golf, easier to play and more inviting to novices. Their proposed rule changes include enlarging the diameter of the hole from 4.25 to 15 inches, allowing a mulligan on every hole, teeing the ball for every shot, and throwing the ball out of a bunker. Just as the golf ball played a central role in starting the boom, Bishop and others hope it might yet play a role in rescuing golf from its current decline. They suggest abandoning restrictions against nonconforming balls in recreational play, allowing for the use of experimental balls engineered to correct hooks and slices. For the moment, however, most golfers reject these changes as crass gimmickry. Curtis Strange, a former US Open champion, speaks for the majority: "I don't want to rig the game and cheapen it. I don't like any of that stuff. And it's not going to happen, either."[27]

Perhaps the secret of making golf fun again rests not in rewriting the rules but in rediscovering what seemed lost for Updike: the harmony between a player, a ball, and a landscape. The subtlety of intention underlying Augusta or any great course designed since the beginning of the golf boom signals a revolution in landscape design bound directly to the evolution of the golf ball. The advent of the gutta-percha and wound balls contributed not only to a widespread conversion of farms and forests to new courses but also to the emergence of more complex architectural visions that enhanced golf as a ludic experience. As bulldozers and modern agronomy gave designers like Bendelow, Ross, and MacKenzie the technical capability to realize these visions, the ancient and accidental beauties of St. Andrews gave way to the ingeniously construed puzzles of Amen Corner. Subtly, the golf ball has terraformed the planet by driving new masses of golfers to claim more acreage for the game and by inspiring the architects of the game to engineer all this land for more fun.

5 HOW THE GOLF BALL WENT BALLISTIC

In his 1933 memoir *The Spirit of St. Andrews,* Alister MacKenzie compares advances in golf balls to advances in the weaponry that would soon lay waste to Europe. During the First World War, he recalls, "experts told us we had got to the limit of flight of a cannonball; then the Germans invented a gun which propelled a shell three times as far as it had ever been sent before. . . . It is often suggested that we have already got to the limit of the flight of a golf ball. I do not believe it, as there is no limit to science."[1] MacKenzie's casual comparison between golf balls and cannonballs suggests an interesting parallel in the way golf balls, armaments, and many other objects came to be designed and constructed, with a vision toward surpassing previous limits through the application of science. While most of the innovations to the golf ball prior to the Second World War were made by accident—Paterson's molding of a golf ball from a gutta-percha mail packaging or Haskell's idle tinkering with rubber twine—ball design in the second half of the twentieth century has been driven by precise laboratory methods practiced by highly trained engineers using synthetic polymers, robotic swing arms, wind tunnels, and high-speed photography. In this respect, the design of modern golf balls, as MacKenzie suggested in 1933, has indeed followed the same path as aeronautics and ballistics.

As a golf ball's most distinctive surface feature, dimples illustrate this general shift from accidental to engineered design. Dimples give golf balls their aerodynamic properties, and subtle variations in dimple design create subtle variations in flight. Unknown in the era of feather balls and early gutta-percha balls, this correlation between a textured surface and better flight properties was itself discovered by accident in the late nineteenth century, when players found that the smooth guttie gained more loft after being nicked and scarred with use. They had fortuitously discovered the Bernoulli Principle at work on balls in flight: irregularities on the ball surface caused lift by pulling air around the spinning ball, reducing air pressure above the ball and increasing pressure below it. Players also found that scoring the surface in different patterns could make the ball fly in different ways and chiseled signature markings in an effort to discover the ideal pattern. Eventually manufacturers took the cue from players and produced textured gutties with raised nubs, or "brambles," on the surface.

These initial accidental discoveries have led to an endless succession of more intentional experiments and adjustments. Following the invention of the Haskell ball, manufacturers found that concave dimples created more spin and better flight than convex brambles. Smaller, deeper dimples create a lower flight trajectory, while larger, shallow dimples create higher flight. More recently, octahedral patterns have given way to icosahedral patterns, which present the same face to the air no matter which way the ball spins. Tetraicosahedral, deltahedral, and dodecahedral patterns have followed, all promising truer flight. Among regulation balls on the current market, Kasco's Kira series have the fewest dimples with 252, while MacGregor's Lady Distance 458 and MX Distance have the most with 458. The Ecoviepure has the most unusual pattern, with striking rosettes formed by an artful arrangement of pentagonal, hexagonal, and elliptical dimples.

The materials used in golf balls have likewise become highly specialized and very different from the organic stuff—feathers, hide, and sap—used in featheries and gutties. In the twentieth century, polyurethanes became what gutta-percha was in the nineteenth century: a thermoplastic miracle goo with seemingly innumerable consumer applications, including foam packing, foam seating, foam insulation, superglue, sealant, spandex, gaskets, hoses, bulletproof vests, car parts, computer parts, television parts, rollercoasters, roller skates, skateboards, surfboards, shoes, and simulated wood. DuPont initiated the use of synthetic resins in golf balls with Surlyn, a polymer that replaced balata, the softer, less resistant natural resin used for ball covers. In this sense, Surlyn represents the completion of the evolution of the golf ball from an object molded from organic substances to an object synthesized by molecular engineering.

Like the gutta-percha balls of the Victorian era, polyurethane balls have emerged in concert with a larger economic and technological ascendance. At the same time that DuPont began to produce Surlyn for golf ball covers, the company built and operated a plant for the production of the hydrogen bomb and created a range of synthetic materials for the American space program—a connection fortuitously suggested in the film *Dr. Strangelove*, when the unhinged Colonel Ripper, bent on defending his airbase from those who would stop him from starting a Third World War, pulls a machine gun from his golf bag and sends golf balls bounding, in the midst of Armageddon, around his office bunker. The Surlyn website could indeed convince us that the product might be used for space capsules as well as golf balls:

> DuPont Surlyn ionomer resins are a family of high-performance ethylene copolymers containing acid groups partially neutralized using metal salts such as zinc, sodium and others. The result is an ionically strengthened thermoplastic with enhanced physical properties versus conventional plastics. The DuPont manufacturing process for Surlyn enables highly tailored combinations of pro-perties: outstanding resilience, broad hardness and stiffness range, and excellent resistance to cuts and abrasions.[2]

In other words: better golfing through chemistry.

In the span of the century between the discovery of gutta-percha and the development of Surlyn, ball manufacturing has changed radically. Using an iron spike to wad feathers in a leather sack has given way to "high-performance ethylene polymers." "Technology" has itself become a golf commodity. On the website for its series of Z-Star balls, Srixon promises "Performance driven by technology" and introduces three such "revolutionary" advances, all branded and proprietary: a high grip "Spin Skin" coating for increased spin control; a new "Speed Dimple" pattern to reduce drag and air resistance; and an "advanced Neo Energetic Gradient Growth core" for greater power and velocity on long shots.[3] As MacKenzie sensed in the irrevocable technological advances in the game, the golf ball has become something like a ballistic missile, a cousin to Cold War weaponry by virtue of its molecularly engineered polyurethane DNA.

6 HOW THE GOLF BALL REACHED DÉTENTE

As "golf ball applications" like those integrated into the formidable Srixon Z-Star continue to "drive performance" to further limits, the impulse to protect the game's traditions through the regulation of ball construction becomes correspondingly stronger. Advocates for these traditions point to the potentially disastrous effects of making golf balls that fly, as Alister MacKenzie said, like cannonballs. Hyperextended courses and the resulting slow play, bloated maintenance budgets, higher costs for course managers and players, and diminishing interest among new players could, ultimately, lead to the slow disintegration of the sport—a trend now evidenced in the declining number of golfers. While a new kind of golf ball spurred the growth of the game more than a century ago, today's engineered golf balls now push it to what the course architect Bob Cupp describes as "self-annihilation."[1]

In a press conference following the 2013 Open Championship, Jack Nicklaus leveled a direct indictment against the modern golf ball. "If we went back and left equipment alone but changed the golf ball and brought it back [to previous performance standards]," Nicklaus said, "you played a shorter golf course, not only from the Tour standpoint would it be good, but a shorter golf course all through the game would mean less maintenance cost, less cost to play the game, quicker play, less land, less fertilizer, less everything, which would make the game more economical."[2]

If we "went back," though, how far would we go? As early as the turn of the twentieth century, the problems Nicklaus identifies had already begun to appear at the start of the golf boom. In 1897, the winner of the long drive contest at the Women's Amateur drove her guttie 137 yards; ten years later the winner of the same contest drove her Haskell ball 220 yards.[3] Alarmed by this new ballistic evidence, Alister MacKenzie recommended the universal adoption of the "floater," a larger, lighter ball that demands more imaginative shots. He laments the state of the game in the era that Nicklaus now idealizes, drawing the same connection between the long ball and slow play: "today many are trying to obtain a temporary advantage by buying the latest far-flying ball on the market. . . . I am firmly convinced that a floater would, in the long run, give more lasting pleasure. It would restore much of the old finesse and skill of the game."[4] MacKenzie argues that the "rubber cored ball," has "spoilt" many courses by obviating the strategic choices posed by the design. For instance, the wound ball allowed players to cut many doglegs with long drives. As MacKenzie explains, doglegs equalize holes for players of varied abilities, making strategy more important than length.[5] MacKenzie saw 7,000 yards as a critical threshold, beyond which the integrity of design, and the game itself, suffers.[6]

Shortly after the appearance of the Haskell ball, the USGA heeded such warnings and imposed limits to preserve the integrity of course strategy and shot making. On January 1, 1932, after a series of trials with larger and lighter balls, the USGA established the dimensions of the regulation ball that remain in place today: no less than 1.68 inches in diameter, and no more than 1.62 ounces in weight. The regulation allowed ball makers to continue experiments with larger or lighter balls, but not smaller or heavier ones. Because it made no restriction on the materials used to construct the balls, golf ball "ballistics" research shifted from experimenting with size and weight to experimenting with new kinds of plastics and layering. In this way, the USGA forged a détente between ball makers and golf purists, allowing for continued innovations in ball design while protecting the courses from the imminent cannonade of newer, better golf balls. The imposition of this limit represents the first formal check against the imperative of greater distance, which has motivated ball design since the end of the nineteenth century. For MacKenzie and the USGA, the modern golf ball, like Xi's Coke bottle in *The Gods Must Be Crazy*, had become an object of dubious repute that had to be constrained and made to "conform" to an increasingly rigorous and articulate ethical standard about what the game means and how it should be played. In this sense, the evolution of the golf ball has forced golfers to define and defend traditions taken for granted until the turn of the twentieth century.

Some, like Nicklaus, continue to believe that golf's governing organizations should constrain golf ball technology even further with the introduction of a uniform competition ball. As USGA president in 1978 and 1979, Frank "Sandy" Tatum likewise favored a larger, lighter "balloon ball" that could not fly more than 280 yards. In a 2002 interview, Tatum makes the same argument that MacKenzie made in 1933: further regulating the ball would "put shot-making values back into the game," preserve the relevance of older, shorter courses, and obviate the imperative for physical power and athletic ability that now characterizes professional play.[7] In the last decade since the introduction of the Titleist Pro V1 and other highly engineered, state-of-the-art balls, average driving distance on the PGA Tour has increased by nearly 20 yards.[8] In response to a problem that, for Nicklaus and others, seems to be getting worse, Gary Wiren, a PGA Master Professional and author of the *PGA Manual of Golf*, renews the familiar plea for constraint, writing more explicitly on what MacKenzie, Tatum, and Nicklaus also suggest—that golf balls now threaten to destroy golf:

> Controlling the ball's distance is essential to maintaining the *essence* of the game. *Nothing would destroy the game of golf faster than to encourage the use of golf balls that travel*

appreciably farther. If that were to happen, present length courses would no longer offer the same challenge. Having to again lengthen courses would: 1) extend the time of play, 2) require more land for facilities and 3) cost more dollars in maintenance, all of which are problems, even with the present length.[9]

Merion Golf Club in Ardmore, Pennsylvania, has become a widely known case study in the destructive trends that concern Wiren. After Lee Trevino defeated Nicklaus in the 1971 US Open on the East Course at Merion, he praised the course for the challenge it presented: "The thing that intrigues me more about this golf course than most others is that it's a proven fact that you can have a golf course that's under 7,000 yards long and bring a US Open to it and still challenge a golf professional. . . . It shows you that you don't really have to build a golf course that's . . . 7,600 yards, 8,000 yards long. You can still build something on 115 acres which will challenge the best."[10] But Merion would host only one other US Open in the next four decades until it expanded from 6,500 to 7,000 yards to host the 2013 US Open. While intending to diminish the importance of distance as a mandate for competition, Trevino's comment ironically predicted the obsolescence of a course that evoked the heyday of Bobby Jones rather than beckoning the long bombers who would dominate the tour in subsequent decades. As Tom Doak observes, however, simply lengthening old courses like Merion is a clumsy solution; stretching holes destroys their "philosophy" and distorts the strategic options embedded in the original design. Rather than renovating and lengthening old courses, Doak, like Nicklaus, advocates for new ball standards to impose a stricter limit on maximum distance and restore integrity to older designs.[11]

In his autobiography, *My Story*, Nicklaus cites Merion as the primary illustration of the way new balls threaten to destroy the game through the unsustainable extension of golf courses. He details his concern about the distances possible with constantly evolving golf balls and worries that the "great old courses" have become obsolete, "less interesting to play."[12] Nicklaus renews MacKenzie's and Tatum's arguments for a uniform ball, as well as a reduced distance standard for commercial balls, which would restore the challenge of old courses and place renewed emphasis on player skill rather than equipment. In advocating for reduced distance standard, Nicklaus defies the industry. "There is no question this would create uproar among the ball-makers," he writes, "who hate the idea of distance restriction for many reasons, among them the invalidation of the 'ours-is-longest' sales pitch (which is baloney anyway), and the frustration of the average golfer's desire to play the same ball as his or her hero uses."[13]

As venerable courses like Merion stretch out, and new courses are built to dwarf the old courses, golf consumes more land, more water, more habitat, and more dollars. As Doak explains, contemporary course designers have to consider environmental problems that earlier generations of designers did not, including the use of treated wastewater and the potential damage to local wildlife and habitats by course construction and maintenance.[14] The sport that often claims nature as its first architect has now become the target of environmental activists who see golf courses not as preserves of natural beauty, as MacKenzie did, but rather as bloated juggernauts of consumption and waste.

These environmental issues have led some designers to return to the notion of "finding" courses rather than engineering them—the architectural approach of MacKenzie and others, who sought to adapt golf to the land, not vice versa. Doak returns to the earliest courses as models for contemporary, ecologically aware designers. He believes that St. Andrews, for example, has survived the advance of technology to remain the "ultimate thinking course." The Old Course furnishes Doak with a model for his own design at Pacific Dunes in Bandon, Oregon. Like MacKenzie, Doak advocates the use of natural topography in course design and believes that natural "undulation," which both pleases the eye and poses strategic challenges, "is the soul of the game."[15]

With courses like Doak's Pacific Dunes, designers seek to change the dominant paradigm for constructing and maintaining golf courses, which no longer need to be exercises in economic and environmental "self-annihilation." In each of their respective eras, MacKenzie, Nicklaus, and Doak recognize the same problems arising from technological change, and all of them seek to preserve the integrity of golf through the regulation of the golf ball. In golf, ethics has responded to science as the ball becomes contested ground in the debate about the identity and future of the game.

7 HOW THE COURT DECIDED CUSTODY OF THE GOLF BALL

Since the advent of the wound ball, advances in aerodynamics and chemistry have prompted efforts by the game's guardians to protect traditions established when golf was played, and golf balls were made, in an agricultural world. On one side we hear ball manufacturers promising greater distance through science; on the other there are protests of tradition, wary that unrestrained science could, like Frankenstein's monster, destroy the game.

This perennial conflict manifested itself in an obscure but illuminating patent infringement suit brought before a British High Court in 1905. The Haskell Golf Ball Company, which had lately come to control the market with its wound ball design, alleged that Richard Hutchison and John Main were manufacturing their Springvale golf balls using the same design that Haskell had patented. The defense claimed that the covers of the Springvale balls were derived from vulcanized India rubber, not gutta-percha, and therefore did not infringe on the Haskell patent, which specified a gutta-percha cover. More importantly, the defense challenged Haskell's claim to "novelty," arguing that wound balls like Haskell's had been manufactured, traded, and played by Scottish golfers for decades prior to the patent. The witnesses for the defendants included a circle of golf "enthusiasts" who claimed that the wound ball was not invented by Coburn Haskell at the Goodrich factory in Akron, but rather at St. Andrews, in Old Tom Morris's workshop.

The most persuasive of the defense witnesses proved to be "Captain" Duncan Stewart, the architect of the hallowed Machrihanish golf course and a friend of Morris, in whose "shed" Stewart claimed to have made wound balls thirty years before Haskell secured the patent. The judge cites Stewart's testimony in his decision:

> Captain Stewart was an enthusiast, continually experimenting in the making of golf balls. He made many kinds. Amongst them was a ball of wound rubber thread enclosed in a cover of gutta-percha. He made these from about 1871 to as late as 1879. In the course of those years he arrived at what he considered to be a satisfactory ball. In his view it was the best ball he made, or knew. He played with it himself; he gave it to friends. . . . Stewart and not the Patentee, was the first and true inventor. . . .

The Plaintiffs fail, I think, on the issue of novelty. Under these circumstances the action must fail, and I dismiss it with costs.[1]

Alister MacKenzie fondly remembers the decision, looking back on his friendship with "Commander Stuart" and, perhaps, embellishing the court record in his memory. As MacKenzie recalls, Stewart, like Haskell himself, discovered the wound ball by happy accident: "He told me that he had conceived the idea from seeing strings of elastic protruding from ladies' elastic sided boots. He thought that if similar elastic strands were strung tightly round a central core and covered with gutta percha a ball of great resiliency could be made." MacKenzie adds: "During his evidence, so he told me, the judge asked him, 'Can you tell me, Commander Stuart, of any man except you and Tom Morris who played with your rubber cored ball in those days?' 'Yes,' he replied, 'your own father, sir.' This clinched the case against the Haskell people."[2]

What was at stake in this case for the Haskell Ball Company—the exclusive right to manufacture a revolutionary type of golf ball—differed from what was at stake for Stewart, Morris, and MacKenzie: the right to claim native genius. Stewart testified that, unlike Haskell, he never sought to profit from his experiments with the wound ball, nor did he aim to secure a patent and make his discovery public. In fact he attempted to conceal his design from rival golfers who, he worried, might reproduce the wound ball and shoot better scores. Stewart was equally competitive in the courtroom where, rather than monetary compensation, he simply wanted to wrest the trophy of "novelty," origination, from the Ohio tire manufacturers and restore it to its rightful place at St. Andrews.

The case indeed raises intriguing questions about the custody of the game. If the wound ball signifies the advent of modern golf, then was it conceived in Tom Morris's shed or a tire factory in Akron? Who really owned the game? We find here the same competing claims of "novelty" that we find in the alternate accounts of the invention of the gutta-percha ball. Paterson and Stewart, ingenious and irrepressible golfers, stand against the industrial machinery of the W.T. Henley Telegraph Company and B.F. Goodrich. Although the court decided in favor of Scotland's native genius and permitted Hutchison and Main to continue manufacturing Springvale balls, the decision would not change the fact that golf balls were then, as now, produced in factories through industrial processes, nor did it change the fact that managers of rubber factories had inherited the golf ball and, in some respects, the game itself, from sages like Tom Morris and Duncan Stewart.

Understanding the latent significance in this forgotten patent suit means seeing the golf ball as a microcosm of global economic history bound in a polyurethane nutshell. The featherie was produced from bull's hide and bird feathers, materials readily available to a craftsman laboring in a largely pastoral world. The guttie and Haskell ball were produced from natural or synthetic latex, materials available only to industrial manufacturers. Objects that could once be created from things collected from a local farmyard were now created from substances collected through global trade networks stretching from Malaysian jungles to London factories. Nonetheless, these early factory-made balls retained at their core a hidden residue of the old organic world—honey, hair, blood, soil, wood.

Today, modern golf balls are produced entirely from synthetic polymers, created by highly specialized chemical engineers working in corporate research labs supported by a financial apparatus involving mass marketing, player sponsorships, and endless branding. While Tom Morris or Duncan Stewart could cobble a featherie, a guttie, or a wound ball in their workshop, no golfer today, no matter how clever, could go out to his garage and make anything like the Titleist Pro V1 or the Srixon Z-Star. In this important respect, the golf ball and, consequently, the player's experience of the game have changed. The average golfer today, unlike Captain Stewart or Old Tom, has almost no practical knowledge about the material dimensions of his ball or the means of its production. Certainly the "ionomer mantle" guarantees "greater distance off the tee," but what is "ionomer" and why does it make a golf ball go? What is "high grip spin coating"? What is a "Neo Energetic Gradient Growth core"? The moral victory of golf's old guard over the factory managers in *Haskell v. Hutchison* preserved a fleeting sense that players, and not assembly lines and laboratories, still made golf. This nostalgia for a preindustrial experience leads Alister MacKenzie to beatify "Commander Stuart" and, in the same way, leads us to beatify Alister MacKenzie.

But there is a paradox in modern primitivism. The Stone Age Bushmen seem isolated and peaceful because they *do not* live in the Stone Age but rather in a world where people throw Coke bottles out of airplanes. With his black Nike hat and his sculpted physique, Tiger Woods, striding the fairway in grim pursuit of another victory, only adds to the mystique of gray-bearded Tom Morris, one hand in the pocket of his tweed coat and the other on the hickory shaft of his mashie niblick. Because we have the former, we need the latter. In this curious recursive process, tradition is produced by the same changes that seem to threaten it. Even as we buy golf balls engineered on a molecular level, created by the same processes that created the bomb, bulletproof vests, superglue, and spandex, we sanctify tradition, treating the rules that protect it as scripture, the players who embody it as saints, and the old courses where it lives as hallowed ground. At the first tee, no golfer would not trade his Srixon Z-Star for a featherie, but neither would he betray the tradition that the hatful of feathers signifies.

8 HOW THE GOLF BALL BECAME THE #1 BALL IN GOLF

In 2002, the Acushnet Company, makers of the venerable Titleist golf balls, asked a Florida district court for an injunction against Nitro Leisure Products, a company, at the time of the suit, that made nearly five million dollars a year recovering and selling used golf balls. In addition to "recycled" balls—those found in good condition and requiring only washing and buffing before they can be repackaged and resold—Nitro also sold "refurbished" balls, those found with scuffs, stains, and scratches and requiring the application of new paint and a new manufacturer's trademark. While Acushnet did not object to the sale of the "recycled" golf balls, it argued "Nitro's refurbishing process produces a golf ball that bears no resemblance to a genuine Acushnet product in performance, quality, or appearance." Acushnet further argued that Nitro's refurbishing treatment "so alters the basic composition of Acushnet's golf balls," that Nitro's reapplication of the Titleist brand would deceive the consumer by associating the brand with an inferior product.[1] You can have the balls, Acushnet said, but not the brand.

Like *Haskell v. Hutchison* a century earlier, the case turned on trademark infringement law, which states that "any person who uses the trademark of another, without consent, in a manner that is likely to cause confusion, mistake, or to deceive may be liable in a civil action." The law does not prevent the resale of used goods bearing original trademarks, but it does prevent the use of trademarks on used goods that have been "materially" changed, beyond expected wear and tear. Acushnet argued that the process of removing and reapplying paint and trademarks materially changed the Titleist balls, deceiving consumers who had the right to expect "Titleist" quality.[2]

The court ruled in favor of Nitro, concluding that they had not infringed on Acushnet's trademark. The refurbishing process, the court decided, did not significantly alter the performance of the original ball because the changes were "cosmetic" and not "material." More importantly, the court said, Nitro attached prominent disclaimers both to the packaging and to the balls themselves, stating that they had been stripped, repainted, and restamped, and that they might exhibit "performance variations" from new balls. Citing the disclaimer, the court ruled that Nitro did not deceive or confuse consumers by reaffixing the brand to the refurbished balls, which were still materially Titleists.

As in *Haskell v. Hutchison*, which decided the proprietary status of the wound ball and marked an important transition in the evolution of the game, *Nitro v. Acushnet* likewise represents an interesting landmark in the way we define the ball in both legal and ontological terms. Each case posited a new answer to the deceptively simple question: what is a golf ball? *Haskell v. Hutchison*, though decided in favor of the St. Andrews artisans over the B.F. Goodrich industrialists, marked the arrival of the golf ball as an industrial commodity and a new phase in the social and economic dimensions of the game.

Nitro v. Acushnet addresses a subtler ontological question. Does the golf ball consist of a material object of paint and plastic, or does it consist of a trademark, a brand, and a logo? Has the industrial commodity defined by *Haskell v. Hutchison* given way to the more fluid representation of product branding? In essence, has the ball become identical with its brand? The Florida district court said that a golf ball consists of its material being, the glob of polyurethane, the weight of matter beneath the paint and the emblem that carries the value of market price and social prestige. For this reason, they ruled, Nitro could strip the paint and the image and still call the object "Titleist." Because Nitro did not materially alter the polyurethane glob, it could efface and reapply the brand without infringing on Acushnet's hallowed trademark.

The decision of the Florida court was affirmed on appeal in 2003, but a dissenting opinion from one of the appellate judges signals a transition in our understanding of the ontological status of a golf ball or any other commodity. The dissenting judge argued that the essence of a golf ball rests not in its material form but rather in its name and the nonmaterial qualities the name conveys:

> The district court found Nitro's process not to be "intrusive," in that it "does not remove the dimples on the balls, nor does it take off the cover of the ball." The issue, however, is Nitro's right to re-apply the Titleist and Pro V1 trademarks to the repainted balls. . . . In an ever more complex commercial economy, it is increasingly important to preserve standards of quality and confidence. Trademark law carries this burden. The record states that the Titleist balls are the premium balls in this market, and are recognized by the golfing public as of high and consistent quality and dependability. The producer of these products is entitled by law to protect the reputation and the value of its marks.[3]

The legal question of whether a golf ball's identity lies in its matter or its brand marks a radically new conception of the golf ball, which, despite the ruling against Acushnet, now consists not only of the physical materials used to construct the object but also of the assemblage of abstract meanings and values contained in the brand. The ball has gained an immaterial, fetishistic being.

Current ball design and marketing incorporate brand identity in ways that would have been incomprehensible to

John Gourlay, Robert Paterson, or Coburn Haskell, using an alchemy of colors and nomenclature to invoke a range of abstract values about tradition, social status, and gender. Acushnet appeals primarily to the tradition it defended against Nitro. "There's a difference between a golf ball and the #1 ball in golf," the Titleist website says. "For over 75 years, Titleist golf balls have been designed and manufactured by Titleist associates and in Titleist manufacturing facilities." Titleists come almost exclusively in traditional white. Of some sixty varieties on the current market, forty-nine are white, nine are yellow, and two are orange. Acushnet's advertisement for its flagship product, the Titleist Pro V1, appeals not only to tradition but also to "better performance through technology":

> Tour-proven around the globe, the new Titleist Pro V1 golf ball . . . utilizes a softer compression ZG process core technology, features a responsive ionomeric casing layer, and an improved high-performance Urethane Elastomer cover system with a 352 tetrahedral dimple design.

Most golfers probably don't know what a ZG process, an ionomeric casing, or a tetrahedron is, but they do know they add up to a Titleist.

Dunlop's extensive Srixon series features a conservative palette of white, yellow, and orange, similar to Acushnet's, but also includes one pink ball, the Soft Feel Lady. The Srixon website invests the "SF Lady" with an identity that appeals both to technical sophistication and feminine sensibility:

The Soft Feel Lady brings all of the success of Srixon's distance technology to a golf ball specifically designed for women. The super-soft Energetic Gradient Growth core enables low to moderate swing speed golfers to generate impressive ball speed while maintaining excellent feel. . . . Also available in Passion Pink!

Kasco manufactures balls in every primary and secondary color of the visible spectrum; its Kira series is available not only in white, yellow, and orange, but also in red, blue, green, purple, and, of course, pink. Relatively new to the market, Kasco further distinguishes itself from the traditionalism of Acushnet and Dunlop with promises of excitement and novelty. Its summer 2013 catalogue says: Kira, achieving 'visibility,' is a nice ball to look at, fun to own, and enjoyable to play with." More than just fun, though, Kasco makes an obligatory appeal to science: "Kira is not a mere tinted ball. Ultraviolet rays are transformed to visible rays due to fluorescent pigments, achieving 'visibility' as the eye tends to catch these rays to a greater extent."[4] Emphasizing "visibility" with scare quotes, Kasco seems eager to call attention to itself—the eye-catching newcomer to a market dominated by old rubber conglomerates like Bridgestone and Dunlop. While Acushnet appeals to conservatism and conformity, Kasco appeals to trends toward greater flamboyance and expressiveness, as golf expands beyond the country club gates into a more diverse demographic.

As golf becomes more diverse, so, too, do golf balls, particularly as gendered objects. For women, the "softness" and "feel" promised by the SF Lady and other brands seem to offer the "control" necessary for confident play without imposing an uncomfortable masculine label. Some brands marketed to female players sound like commercials for women's razors: the Srixon Soft Feel Lady, of course, the Kolwin Lady Soft, and the Precept Lady iQ. Some golf balls marketed to men, on the other hand, sound like the names of professional wrestlers: the Callaway Diablo and Warbird, the TaylorMade Lethal and Rocketballz, the Snake Eyes SDF Extreme. Many others bear corporate neologisms with the vague and sexless tone of a new line of luxury cars, the products with which they share so much commercial time during televised golf tournaments: Altus, Excedian, Ignio, Inesis, Everio, Newing, Rextar, XD Aero, Proto 3.

If we listen closely to the language of golf ball branding, we hear the odd poetry that resonates in all advertising: the mellifluous but meaningless names, the metaphoric yoking of a material object with deep emotional desires. Subliminal messages seem to border on the territory of enchantment, where a certain ball, with a certain name, a certain color, and some magic words—*Ionomer! Elastomer! Tetrahedron!*—can appeal to something deep within us and make us want it.

9 HOW THE GOLF BALL GOT SO COOL

Golfers often make palimpsests of their balls, inscribing over the ubiquitous manufacturer's brand an idiosyncratic personal mark that infuses the object with individual meaning. In play, these marks distinguish somebody's Titleist, Bridgestone, or Nike from somebody else's, and a straight black line drawn on a ball's equator often helps to align a put. Usually, though, something more inheres in these personal markings, which often seem more talismanic than practical. Various configurations of red dots, blue dots, green dots, black dots, straight lines, crossed lines, circles and squares and triangles, single initials, double initials, and signatures often yield to more allusive hieroglyphics, etched as much to invest a ball with hermetic power as to distinguish it from its homogeneous peers.

On the PGA Tour, many golfers create their own unofficial heraldry. Rickie Fowler, famous for his orange tournament clothing, makes a large orange dot on his ball. Nick Faldo inscribes a "6" for his six major championships.

Graeme Storm decorates the logo on his Titleist with a storm cloud and lightning bolt. Some golfers use their ball to declare their national pride. Nick O'Hern and Jason Day, for example, use kangaroos for their native Australia. Adam Scott, another Aussie, uses the Southern Cross constellation that adorns the nation's flag. Darren Clarke honors Northern Ireland with a green shamrock. Graham DeLaet stencils the red Canadian maple leaf on his Titleists, and Brett Quigley marks his ball with an army-green sharpie in tribute to American soldiers. Others show loyalty to their alma mater: David Toms makes a purple dot for Louisiana State, Jonathan Byrd makes an orange dot for Clemson, and Ben Crane draws a yellow circle with a green border for the University of Oregon. Still others carry thoughts of their family on the course. Jim Furyk inscribes a "58" on his TaylorMade Penta TP, the sum of the birthdays of his wife and kids. Louis Oosthuizen uses the initials "LNJS," the first initials of himself, his wife, and his two daughters.[1]

Other golfers are just plainly superstitious, using a particular color or arrangement of dots that seemed to serve them well in a past tournament. Keegan Bradley draws a large red "V" for victory on his Srixon, and Brandt Snedeker marks his Bridgestone with a single green dot for the green jacket he hopes to win one day at the Masters. As a superstition or a test of nerves, Tiger Woods reputedly draws a single vector, perfectly straight, on his Nike ball while trotting amid the throng from the practice range to the first tee. Fredrik Jacobsen is superstitious of superstition. He blots out the numbers on his Callaways to avoid the temptation of thinking that numbers matter, a psychological tactic that seems to match his tendency to wear only white for tournament play—a color, perhaps, to keep him from thinking that colors matter.[2]

In the mystical milieu of Michael Murphy's *Golf in the Kingdom*, Shivas Irons, the resident mage of Burningbush, recognizes that symbols and brands convey the latent power of abstract ideas. They capture consumers with "heraldry and pageants and cunning toorns," Shivas says. "Some o' them have stumbled right into the first principles of occultism. . . . Put a symbol into the mind and it takes on a life of its own. . . . Strong images are like seeds in the soul. . . . When they're planted there they grow, start havin' a powerful effect."[3] Wherein resides this curious belief that making a mark on a golf ball converts it into a kind of talisman, capable somehow of warding off misfortune and conferring success?

Like Murphy, the novelist William Gibson recognizes the hidden power of symbols, though he locates its source in subliminal messages rather than in "occultism." In Gibson's novel *Pattern Recognition*, Cayce Pollard works as a freelance consultant for advertising firms to assess the potential for new brands and logos to take root in consumer consciousness. She's a "cool hunter," different from other marketing experts because instinct, not data, guides her judgments. She reacts viscerally, feeling excited, flat, or nauseous when presented with a proposed logo. The marketing guru Hubertus Bigend regards Cayce's ability as a heightened sensitivity to the unconscious appeal in all advertising. The most effective strategies, Bigend explains, subvert the conscious will of the consumer, working as a kind of enchantment to invest objects with irrational but irresistible appeals. He offers Cayce a short lesson in Marx's notion of commodity fetishism, updated with evolutionary psychology. The limbic system, he says, is the "seat of instinct. The Mammalian brain. Deeper, wider, beyond logic. That is where advertising works. . . . And makes us buy things."[4] Cayce's ability strikes us as a highly specialized gift, perhaps even a form of extrasensory perception, but, as Bigend knows, all consumers behave according to the same irrational instincts, even if they're not as attuned to them as Cayce is.

If Cayce Pollard wanted to hunt for a cool golf ball, she would probably consider the confident superiority of the Titleist Pro V1, the technical complexity of the Srixon U-6, or the offbeat "visibility" of the polychromatic Kiras. Ultimately, though, her nostalgic affection for Cold War chic would lead her to the Penfold Hearts, the only ball cool enough for James Bond. In *Goldfinger*, the golf match between 007 and his nemesis begins harmlessly, "a shilling a hole." On the seventeeth, however, when Bond reveals that he has a Nazi gold bar, Goldfinger raises the stakes: the gold bar, or its equivalent of five thousand pounds, to the winner of the last two holes. Goldfinger loses his ball, a Slazenger 1, in the rough, but his bodyguard, serving as his caddie, surreptitiously drops another Slazenger 1 and claims to have found the first ball. Bond turns the tables, however, by switching Goldfinger's ball for a Slazenger 7 on the seventeenth green. He intentionally misses his last putt on the eighteenth, allowing Goldfinger to claim a momentary victory before springing the trap. With his usual suave and cunning, 007 observes that Goldfinger has played the wrong ball. "You play a Slazenger 1, don't you? This is a Slazenger 7." He picks up his own ball. "Here's my Penfold Hearts. You must have played the wrong ball somewhere on the eighteenth fairway." According to the rules, Bond wins the hole and the match, and Goldfinger curses in frustration. As they leave the club together, Bond reveals the Slazenger 1 he filched on the seventeenth green, tosses it to the bodyguard and quips, "I believe this is yours."[5]

As Penfold Clubs, Diamonds, and Spades slid into obscurity, *Goldfinger* lifted the Hearts to "shaken, not stirred" fame. Half a century later, the Penfold Hearts has lost none of its allure. In 2008, Penfold produced a limited collector's set of the balls to celebrate the centennial of Ian Fleming's birth, available in the United Kingdom for £50. On eBay, vintage Penfolds command high prices: $50 for a single Hearts and nearly $300 for a full box including the other Penfold balls.

Understanding what makes the Penfold Hearts cool, and maybe what makes us draw cool things on golf balls, means exploring the ramifications of *Nitro v. Acushnet* and tracing the evolution of the golf ball from an object to an idea. How do we invest material objects with abstract meanings and convert them into fetishes for sex, power, or luck? Before 007 or Gibson or Murphy, Karl Marx expressed both fascination and concern with the apparent power of commodities to embody, or reify, human relations and abstract values—the power of a diamond ring, for example, to embody love, or the power of a Titleist to embody good taste and respect for tradition. In order to understand this capacity for "perceptible" objects to take on "imperceptible" qualities, Marx ventures into the "mist-enveloped regions of the religious world" and draws an analogy between commodities and primitive fetishes. For the believer, the fetish is a physical object endowed with supernatural life. "So it is in the world of commodities," Marx concludes, where money and marketing can enchant a merely useful thing and make it cool.[6]

As its suit against Nitro suggests, Acushnet has sought to capitalize on its privileged place in golf tradition and market its own coolness as a commodity in itself, almost separate from the balls. The company, like most others, now offers custom imprinting to individuals and organizations who pay to have their name stamped on new Titleists. Instead of drawing your initials, the logo of your company, or the insignia of your alma mater on your ball with a Sharpie, you can have Acushnet do it for you at the authentic "Titleist manufacturing facilities," making your ball that much cooler. "In golf and in business, it's wise to choose a strong partner," the website advises. "Align yourself, your company or your country club with the best. Choose Titleist custom golf balls and make a great impression."[7] The site pictures the iconic Titleist 1 branded with the logos of luxury hotel chains, luxury car companies, and luxury golf resorts, promising a kind of sympathetic magic: wealth breeds wealth. Win friends and influence people with your golf ball.

With these corporate emblems, and with personal marks invoking nations, schools, families, lucky numbers or auspicious icons, golf balls become tokens of social prestige, talismans of good fortune, cool commodities. Affixed to an object, a symbol opens the distance between utility and value. A golf ball transcends its immediate purpose—transcends its being as a glob of plastic—and becomes a harbor for identity, an avatar of the self. With this leap from thing to idea, we reach the boundary between our outward exploration of the golf ball as a material object and our inward exploration of the golf ball as a phenomenon, a mode of experience. The capacity for a golf ball to embody the values invested in it with brands and markings reveals its immaterial dimension, its power to interact not only with club and turf but also with the psyche. If the physical composition of the ball resembles that of a miniature planet, its psychic presence is like a belt of radiation or gravity surrounding the planet, exerting an invisible but palpable influence on whatever enters its field of effect.

PART TWO

IN: PHENOMENON

10 HOW THE GOLF BALL VANISHES BEFORE YOUR EYES

In the last two or three decades, local newspapers from Scotland to California have documented at least eight cases of accidental death as a result of being hit by a golf ball. The victims ranged in age from 10 to 69, and the fatal shots came from as near as 10 yards and as far as 200 yards. In at least one case, the ball caromed off a tree before striking the victim.[1] In 1999, forensic tests to determine the injuries that a flying golf ball might inflict concluded that speed and distance matter less than the point of impact on the body. The temporal areas of the skull, the tests found, are most vulnerable. The immediate cause of death, according to the study, was likely to be severe concussion, hemorrhaging, and swelling in the brain.[2] In every documented case, the victim was struck on the side or back of the head. Sometimes death was sudden; sometimes it came after several days.

The science writer Brian Kaye felt inspired, like Paul on the road to Damascus, to write his study of projectile physics, *Golf Balls, Boomerangs, and Asteroids*, after he was nearly killed by a flying ball on a golf course in Wisconsin. He recalls: "I was startled to hear a sharp crack as a golf ball narrowly missed my head and hit a tree. . . . As I picked up the innocent-looking little white ball that had rolled away from its encounter with the tree, I noticed its structure with new respect."[3] Just as my own early discovery of the lively properties and geophysical layers of the golf ball prompted me to explore the inner life of the thing, Kaye's encounter with the nearly lethal ball leads him to consider its properties and behavior as a kinetic object, a "missile":

As I contemplated the dimples on the near lethal missile from Wisconsin that lay quietly on my desk in front of me, I resolved to gather together all the science I could find about this interesting missile and all the other missiles used in ball games and related games involving the throwing of objects such as the hammer, the boomerang and the Frisbee. I also began to study more dangerous missiles used in warfare, starting with bows and arrows, and working my way up to guided missiles and antitank shells. Later, as my explorations expanded, I found myself looking into the physics of how biologists introduce small foreign bodies into living cells to develop techniques used in the field of genetic engineering, and the potential damage inflicted by fast, miniature meteorites on spacecraft moving through cosmic dust. I also looked at the potential effect of the earth being hit by asteroids.[4]

The closer one looks at objects, as Timothy Morton suggests, the more other objects appear.

Aligning the golf ball with these other missiles leads us to consider, with Kaye, the kinetic properties that could make it lethal. From the perspective of its engineering and manufacturing, the sole purpose of a golf ball's existence is to get hit by a club. What happens, then, when a ball fulfills this intended purpose? We have already considered the Bernoulli effect created by the dimples, which give the ball lift, hold it in the air, and enable the golfer to control its spin and direction with variations in swing. But what happens at the moment of impact? How does a golf ball take flight and change from a repository of potential energy to a bolt of kinetic energy—a missile?

Compared to balls used in other sports, the golf ball has impressive performance standards. Although measurements vary with the skill of the player and the conditions of play, a ball hit by a professional player travels about 150 miles per hour immediately after impact with the club. The serve of a professional tennis player travels about 120 miles per hour. On impact with a wooden bat or hockey stick, baseballs and pucks rarely exceed 110 miles per hour. A soccer ball or football leaving a kicker's foot can reach 80 or 90 miles per hour. Only racquetballs and jai alai balls consistently match or exceed the top speed of a golf ball.

The moment of impact, Kaye explains, takes us into a level of physical reality where the speeds of phenomena outstrip our ability to perceive them. In the hands of a professional golfer, the head of a club meets the ball at about 110 miles per hour, slightly faster than the average professional baseball player can swing a bat. The duration of the impact is only half a millisecond, a fraction of the duration of a typical photo flash, and an even smaller fraction of the time it takes a housefly, a honeybee, or a hummingbird to flap its wings. A standard camera with a shutter speed of four milliseconds might indeed capture a clear, still image of the beating wings of a humming-bird. Focused on a golf ball at the moment of impact, however, the same camera captures only an elongated white blur, as the ball travels about 30 centimeters in four milliseconds. "The blink of an eye," the expression that we use to describe events that happen too fast for us to see, is about 350 milliseconds, or about one-third of a second, in duration. In the blink of an eye, then, a golf ball travels about 25 meters, or 82 feet.

During that half-millisecond of impact, the seemingly hard golf ball dramatically compresses against the clubface, absorbing the energy of the swing that will propel it 200 or 300 yards into grass, sand, water, or trees. In that time, sound travels only about 17 centimeters. A golfer of average height does not hear the crack of his driver on the ball until 5 or 6 milliseconds after impact, when the ball is already rising a few feet into the air. As Kaye observes, a ball leaving the club accelerates from 0 to 150 miles per hour in half a millisecond, about 10,000 times faster than a high performance sports car.

The energy of impact travels the length of the club from the ball to the hands in about 0.6 milliseconds, slightly longer than the duration of the impact. In other words, the ball has left club by the time the nerves in our fingers register the impact. In the very brief but measurable interlude of one-tenth of a millisecond between impact and sensation, the ball, totally eclipsed from our perception by its instantaneous acceleration, escapes our sight, hearing, and touch. In physical terms, the impact of the club on the ball is a microevent, taking place just below our phenomenological horizon. Very briefly, the ball gets knocked out of existence.

Kaye estimates that it takes about 700 milliseconds, about two-thirds of a second, for the brain to register the impact of club on ball and signal other parts of the body to react to the event. In other words, almost a full second passes before we perceive that we have hit the ball, turn our head toward the fairway, and focus our eyes on the distance where, we hope, we catch sight of the ball arcing into the sky. When the ball veers from our field of vision as a result of a hook or a slice, or the white speck disappears into the background scenery, or the ball travels too far before we can adjust our focus to the distance, then we do not regain sight of the ball until we find it somewhere on the course—or we never regain sight of it. Millions of balls are lost simply because players fail to regain visual contact with the ball after it reenters their perceptual range, after its brief submergence in the subspace of the microevent. "Did you see it?" we ask our playing partners, again and again. "Did you see where it went?"

11 HOW THE GOLF BALL MAKES US FEEL FULFILLED, FOR A MILLISECOND

In *Golf in the Kingdom*, Shivas Irons first shakes Murphy out of his mechanistic, over-determined approach to the game by asking him to think of the ball and the "sweet spot" on the clubface as "belonging together," as "already joined" before the swing. Murphy imagines club and ball in synthesis and makes a perfect strike. Connecting with the ball in this way, Murphy says, is "the very essence of golfing pleasure."[1] Ben Hogan speaks of the same ecstasy of the perfect ball strike. "One of the greatest pleasures in golf," he writes, "is the sensation a golfer experiences at the instant he contacts the ball flush and correctly. He always knows when he does, for then and only then does a distinctive 'sweet feeling' sweep straight up the shaft from the clubhead and surge through his arms and his whole frame."[2]

With an initial glimpse of a club striking a ball, we gain a more definite understanding of what happens in the long, eventful second that contains the swing, the impact, and the ascent of the ball into the air. We can, perhaps, anatomize the elusive phenomenon that many golfers, including Murphy and Hogan, call the "hitting sweet spot" or "getting all of it"—the fleeting but ecstatic sensation of hitting the ball in exactly the right way. In this epiphany, mind, body, club, ball, and landscape phase into a perfect synthesis, if only for half a millisecond.

For Murphy, the sweet spot connecting golfer to ball has a metaphysical dimension that Shivas calls "true gravity." Murphy first reaches this transcendental awareness on the ninth tee at Burningbush, the turning point of his round. "It wasn't much," he writes, "just the tiniest glimpse, but I did seem to see a yellow light around a sea gull swooping in from the sea." On the next hole, he sees a "tiny aura" of violet light around his ball as it rests on the tee, a moment before he hits the sweet spot.[3] Later, Murphy interprets these phenomena as a heightened sense of "the deeper lines of force, the deeper structure of the universe."[4]

Few golfers, if any, have shared Murphy's glimpse of a purple aura around their golf ball before a good shot, but every golfer, even the most feckless duffer, at least occasionally, has felt the ecstasy of a perfect strike. Hitting the sweet spot is a universal experience that connects all golfers through an ephemeral but ineffable joy. What happens inside this epiphany? Can it really allow us a glimpse into the "structure of the universe," or at least the structure of ecstatic experience?

When impact actually occurs, we don't hear it, feel it, or see it. For one tenth of a millisecond, the instant between actual impact and our sensory detection of the event, the ball slips out of existence, as far as our senses know. Our body first registers the event almost unconsciously: the sweet "surge" of energy, as Hogan describes it, traveling from the club head, through the shaft, and into the nerve endings in our fingers, which send an electrical signal to our brain. In this instant, the ball has accelerated from 0 to 150 miles per hour. Five or six more milliseconds pass before we hear the crack. By this time, the ball has begun its flight, angling into the air about two feet in front of us. When our brain has registered the impact, the shock might cause us to blink our eyes involuntarily, an action that requires more than 350 milliseconds. By this time, the ball has traveled 25 meters, or 82 feet, into its trajectory. Another relatively long span of time, about 310 milliseconds, passes before our brain signals the muscles in our neck to turn our head toward the fairway to look for the ball. By this time the ball has begun to decelerate in its flight, but it has nonetheless traveled another 20 meters, or 66 feet. By the time our eyes have adjusted focus along the unconsciously estimated trajectory of the ball, almost a full second has passed since impact, and the ball has travelled 70 meters, or 230 feet, from the tee. From impact until this point, the ball remains hidden to us in its ascendance, no more visible than a speeding bullet. The first second of flight is a brief, strange moment of limbo, in which the flying object slips out of time. When it phases back into our sensory range, we catch it as a tiny, flitting blur against the background of sky or trees. As it continues to decelerate at the peak of its trajectory, it becomes a white dot, more sharply defined. The spin and the dimples induce the Bernoulli effect, and the ball takes on a magical quality, seeming to hover weightlessly in the sky for a shimmering moment before beginning its beautiful, arcing descent back to earth. It falls into a green undulation of fairway, bounds two or three times, and then, finally, rolls in a long and steady path toward the green.

Each of these microevents within the larger assemblage of events we know as "driving a golf ball" is a distinct phenomenon: the imperceptible impact of club and ball, the first shock of the impact felt by the nerves, the sound of the strike in our ears, the involuntary blink, the motor response as the head and body turn forward, the scanning of the air with the eyes, the glimpse of a blur, the crystallization of the ball at its height, the slow and wonderful fall to earth, and the final rest on a green wave of turf—separate epiphenomena experienced as one unitary epiphany. Perhaps the well-known but little understood pleasure of hitting the sweet spot, making perfect contact and achieving the perfect result, derives from this unconscious synthesis of separate phenomena into a single complex experience. The pleasure of a golf shot rises gradually over the span of a few seconds, from a depth of reality beneath all sensation, through distinct levels of unconscious perception, and eventually to the full height of consciousness, as we savor the bliss of watching an object in flight over the landscape. The experience is only momentary but also complex and layered, something like a fine wine that we can taste in more ways than we can articulate. In this perfect coordination of mind and body with physics and aesthetics, maybe it's not too much to say, with Murphy, that we glimpse the deeper structure of the universe, or at least that tiny part of it that makes us feel the fullness of our being.

12 HOW TO CONTROL THE UNRULY GOLF BALL

In order to explore the systems that golfers have devised to capture and replicate the fleeting ecstasy of a fine shot, we can look at three of the most widely read and influential golf instruction books of the century: Bobby Jones's *Golf Is My Game*, Ben Hogan's *Five Lessons*, and Jack Nicklaus's *Golf My Way*. Jones published *Golf Is My Game* in 1961, long after he retired from competition and a debilitating spinal disease forced him to give up the game. The book is part instruction manual and part memoir, anatomizing the techniques that allowed Jones to dominate the game in the 1920s. Although Hogan's *Five Lessons* was published serially in *Sports Illustrated* in 1957, before Jones's book, it claims to offer a more "modern" and "scientific" perspective, presented concisely and convincingly by the most skilled practitioner of his generation. Nicklaus's *Golf My Way*, published in several editions between 1974 and 2005, bridges the gap between

Hogan's era and our own, and has distinction as the most widely consulted golf instruction book by the most successful golfer of any era.

As one who lost control of his body later in life, Jones had come to see golf as an exercise in control, a mechanism involving an exchange of energy between body, club, and ball. Golf, he writes, is a "measure of efficiency," demanding from the golfer the "maximum employment of his physical resources in producing a powerful, accurate contact between club and ball." Like a scientific experiment, a good golf shot is repeatable through "good form," and the golfer himself may become like a well-tuned instrument. "To become a really fine golfer," Jones writes, "a person must have the knowledge of the basic requirements of the proper golf swing and work hard to drill his muscles in the performance of this exacting ritual."[1] Some residue of the Protestant work ethic lingers in Jones's philosophy. Through mechanical repetition, golf might become a "developer of character," creating a "rigid discipline of self" that helps the golfer resist "panic" and maintain "vigilance" on the course and in his life.[2]

Hogan likewise describes golf in scientific terms. Like Jones, he assures the frustrated golfer that achieving a repeatable swing is no more difficult than achieving repeatable results using the scientific method. "Golf," he writes, "seems to bring out the scientist in the person."[3] Hogan illustrates this claim throughout *Five Lessons* with a series of diagrams showing the angles, planes, and vectors interacting within an efficient golf swing. In one of these illustrations, an outline of a golfer's body houses a system of generators, transformers, and wiring, configured to deliver a lightning bolt of energy to the golf ball, which appears in the picture to vaporize on contact. "As this power builds up," Hogan writes, "it is transferred from the body to the arms, which in turn transfer it through the hands to the club head. It multiplies itself enormously with every transfer, like a chain action in physics."[4] This image of the golfer as an electrical powerhouse vividly conveys Hogan and Jones's shared notion of the golf shot as a mechanical process. Later in the book, an image of a golfer stripped of his skin reinforces Hogan's metaphor, as if the generators, transformers, and wires have turned into to graceful torques of muscle, bone, and tendon.

While both Jones and Hogan envision the golf swing as an exercise in physical control, they have different ideas about channeling this control. For Jones, the ball itself represents the core, and the swing is merely a system of energy generated to make this core substance react in the desired way. He attributes his talent to his gradual discovery of "what a golf ball could be made to do and how it had to be struck to make it perform as I wanted it to."[5] Like a diligent scientist, he achieves this discovery through trial and error: "When I hit it one way and it didn't go right, I'd try hitting it another way."[6] He advises his reader that in order to perfect this process he should "put his mind upon striking the ball, rather than upon swinging the club." He reiterates, simply, "the most important thing in golf is hitting the ball."[7]

For Hogan, on the other hand, the most important thing is not hitting the ball but rather, as he writes in capital letters: "A CORRECT, POWERFUL, REPEATING SWING." Hogan considers it a categorical truth: "it is utterly impossible for any golfer to play good golf without a swing that will repeat."[8] While Jones advocates modifying the swing to strike the ball in a particular way, Hogan argues oppositely that a golfer can "hit the ball high, low, draw it, fade it, play sand shots, recoveries, half shots—ALL WITHOUT CHANGING HIS SWING."[9] The impact and flight of the ball are merely incidental results of the primary exercise, the swing.

Jones, on the other hand, believes a good swing will emerge naturally in golfers who concentrate on striking the ball as they might approach chopping wood or throwing stones, without self-consciousness.[10] To this end, the instructional diagrams in *Golf Is My Game* magnify the ball, the angle at which the clubhead strikes it, and the resulting spin, rather than body mechanics emphasized in Hogan's diagrams. In fact, no image of a golfer's body appears in Jones's instructional chapters, while no image of the ball appears in Hogan's diagrams, except as a point of orientation for the stance and swing. The contrasting styles of these instructional diagrams reveal a difference in the way that Jones and Hogan imagine control, but they remain parallel expressions of the same fundamental notion that the game is essentially an exercise of a mechanical system involving the three basic elements of body, club, and ball.

In *Golf My Way*, Nicklaus names both Jones and Hogan as his personal "idols" and models for his own play. In fact, his approach adopts strongest aspects of the two, synthesizing Jones's emphasis on ball striking with Hogan's emphasis on the repeatable, perfectible swing. A drawing near the beginning of the book shows Jones, Hogan, and Nicklaus at the moment of striking the ball, all looking strangely identical.[11] Like Jones, Nicklaus believes that all golfers "get to impact a little differently" but "impact is the bit that matters."[12] He opens the book with the fundamental assertion, like Jones, that the "one purpose" of the swing is "to produce the correct impact of club on ball."[13] The "easy way" to achieve a good golf shot, he claims, "is not a particular pattern of swing but proper impact of club on ball."[14]

At the same time, he says that "Golf's One Unarguable, Universal Fundamental" is keeping your head down, and in this respect he shares Hogan's emphasis on repeatable body mechanics. Seeming to contradict his idea that all golfers swing "a little differently," Nicklaus also says that there is "only one correct way to deliver the club to the ball."[15] A "sound, repeating swing," Nicklaus writes, will serve you as well in fly-fishing as it does in golf, helping you "to cast or to hit closest to your best most consistently."[16] Like *Golf Is My Game* and *Five Lessons*, *Golf My Way* is structured according to what all three golfers identify as the fundamental stages of the golf swing, with chapters on the grip, the stance, the backswing, and the downswing. Of the three books, only Jones's includes a chapter on ball striking.

The differences between these three instruction books are less important than their shared pedagogy of control. Even as Jones focuses on the ball, Hogan focuses on the swing, and Nicklaus synthesizes the two approaches, all of them describe the game as a mechanical process subject to control, if not mastery, through the diligent and systematic application of a few fundamental principles. In all three books, control represents the primary element in the phenomenology of enjoyment, and in this sense, they are not only manuals for lower scoring but also guides for heightened experience. Jones, Hogan, and Nicklaus all agree that no one can enjoy golf if they play it badly, and they all make the same promise to their readers: enhanced enjoyment through enhanced control. The popularity and enduring readership of *Golf Is My Game*, *Five Lessons*, and *Golf My Way* rests in this basic promise. As Jones writes: "In a few minutes' study of the material in this chapter, he can learn as much about the possible means of controlling a golf ball as a boy could learn in years of play."[17]

In *Flow*, Mihaly Csikszentmihalyi identifies one of the essential "elements of enjoyment" as the sense of control over our actions, which acts as a psychological antidote to the constant sense of frustration we feel about all the aspects of our experience that we cannot control—things like hunger and thirst, viruses and tornadoes and poverty, and, finally, our entropic slide toward age, illness, and death. Csikszentmihalyi argues that this perpetual sense of lacking control creates a need for "exercising control" in difficult situations. "Only when a doubtful outcome is at stake, and one is able to influence that outcome," he writes, "can a person really know whether she is in control." Csikszentmihalyi believes that games are particularly enjoyable because they create controlled situations by design, furnishing challenges that are neither too easy nor too difficult, rules systems that replace entropy, and, ultimately, the means for us to gain the affirming feeling of control. He concludes: "This sense of being in a world where entropy is suspended explains in part why flow-producing activities can be so addictive."[18]

Still, the experience of control seems all too ephemeral, just as Jones's glib assurance that reading a few pages of his book can substitute for a lifetime of playing seems disingenuous. In golf as in other experiences, enjoyment is transitory while frustration is perpetual. The same chapter containing Jones's promise about "controlling a golf ball" also relates his exasperation in attempting to use technical advice offered by Harry Vardon in a golf magazine. Since that failure, he says, he has rejected learning any golf skill through "written description" and admits his hesitation in writing his own instruction manual.[19] He was rankled by the sports journalists of his heyday, who called him the "Mechanical Man" of golf, and insists that there is "nothing very contrived or conscious" about his play, which he learned simply by following his mother and father around on the course.[20]

Hogan, who embraces the role of Mechanical Man, nonetheless advocates learning by playing, as Jones does. Like Jones, he senses a contradiction in encouraging his readers to learn by playing, and then writing a book of instructions. Hogan resolves this problem in the same way that Jones does, presenting his book as a shortcut to the knowledge that he has gained through a lifetime of experience. "That is my reason for undertaking this series of lessons," he writes. "To put it briefly, the information I will be presenting is a sifting of the knowledge I've tried to acquire since I first met up with golf when I was 12."[21] Nicklaus also claims that *Golf My Way* represents a precious distillation of lifelong experience. Although his lessons are no less mechanical than those of Jones and Hogan, he is perhaps more candid in his view that no one can achieve the "mechanical perfection," "perfect repetition," and "flawless automation" that *Five Lessons* and many other golf manuals promise. When he opens *Golf My Way* with the caveat, "you cannot automate the golf swing," he sounds like a rueful genius contemplating futile schematics for a cold fusion reactor or a perpetual motion machine. Such miraculous control, the great Jack Nicklaus says, is only a "dream."[22]

13 HOW TO HIT THE GOLF BALL BY NOT HITTING IT

While Jack Nicklaus's instructions for solid ball striking and a repeating swing reach back to the mechanistic approaches of Jones and Hogan, his lingering sense that absolute control of a golf ball is a "dream" also anticipates more recent books that dispense with physical principles and focus instead on ways to improve the "mental game": holistic techniques such as shot visualization, a heightened sense of continuity with the natural environment, and learning to swing intuitively rather than through repetitive training.

Harvey Penick's *Little Red Book*, a miscellany of advice, anecdotes, and nuggets of social and spiritual wisdom compiled in a notebook during his long career as a golf teacher, looks nothing like *Golf Is My Game*, *Five Lessons*, and *Golf My Way*, with their uniform attention to grip, stance, backswing, and downswing. In fact, Penick's book has no structure. One can open it and start reading at any point, as if by intuition.

Penick takes a similarly intuitive approach to the game. In one anecdote, "Hypnotism," he helps a student correct a slice not by telling him to turn his wrists and close the clubface, as Jones, Hogan, or Nicklaus might, but rather by telling him to "make a couple of practice swings without a ball." Penick then puts the ball on the tee, but he tells the student to close his eyes and swing as he did for practice, without the ball. Then, he tells us, the student "hit the prettiest shot you ever saw."[1] The scene seems as improbable as the scene in *Star Wars* where Obi-Wan Kenobi puts blinders on young Luke Skywalker and tells him to deflect the attacks of the training droid without the benefit of sight. Penick later distills this anecdote into the aphorism: "Picture the shot as you would *like* to see it."[2] Or, as Obi-Wan might say: "Use the force." This little story from *The Little Red Book* seems anathema to the doctrine of control that defines golf manuals in the classic style, particularly Jones's intense concentration on the golf ball as the singularity driving the whole dynamic of the swing. For Penick, the golf ball need not exist for one learning to hit it.

Joseph Parent's *Zen Golf* represents a fuller expression of Penick's "Hypnotism," combining principles of sports psychology and Buddhist meditation. Parent draws an immediate distinction between his own ideas and the exercises in physical control that we find in *Golf Is My Game*, *Five Lessons*, and *Golf My Way*. *Zen Golf*, he says, teaches "time-tested mindfulness and awareness techniques and exercises for working with thoughts and emotions, for settling and centering your body and mind, for changing unhelpful habits." We could apply Parent's advice to yoga as easily we can apply it to hitting a golf ball.[3] Like Penick, who teaches his student to envision his perfect shot without seeing the golf ball, Parent suggests taking our eye and our mind off the ball: "If we get 'ball-bound' before we swing, we lose track of the space we're sending the ball into."[4] This visualization of the total "space" of the golf shot encompasses not only the club and the ball, not only the body of the golfer, but also the fairway and green, the course, the planet, and the whole universe.

Although Parent acknowledges the importance of a consistent swing, he believes that sound mechanics flow from a sound mind, and he has little use for the angles, planes, and vectors of traditional golf manuals. "Don't change your swing, change your mind," the Zen master says. "Clear the interference, then trust your own perfect swing and it will give you the most consistent results." He continues: "When I ask golfers the purpose of making a golf swing, most of them answer, 'To hit the ball.' Yet focusing on the ball as the target is a problematic perspective." In the same way, the "intention to 'make sure I make a good swing' is likely to promote mechanical thinking." But, as Parent concludes, "if your purpose is to fulfill an image of the ball flying or rolling to a target, the image fills your mind, and your body swings the club with far less interference."[5]

Parent's philosophy rests on the idea of visualization, that you can realize a good shot simply by imagining it. Instead of packing *Zen Golf* with the instructional diagrams we find in *Golf Is My Game*, *Five Lessons*, and *Golf My Way*, he tells his readers to hold the image of the perfect shot in their mind's eye, much as Shivas instructs Murphy at Burningbush: "Clarity is having an image of the full shot that you intend— where the ball is going to come to rest and how it's going to get there. To do this, take all your calculations and planning and transform them into an image."[6] For Parent, visualization can determine both success and failure: "when we say to ourselves, 'Don't hit the ball into the lake,' the image that appears in our mind is our golf ball flying toward and splashing into the lake." Inevitably, the result follows the image. "That image is the message our body responds to and does its best to produce." Parent warns: "You produce what you fear," but you can also produce what you desire.[7]

Golf in the Kingdom illustrates Parent's lesson that the mind's eye can realize our fears and desires. Murphy's round at Burningbush begins auspiciously with a long, beautiful shot from the first tee, a shot he visualizes before it happens. After teeing up the ball, he writes "a vivid image appeared in my mind's eye, of a turquoise ball traveling down the right side of the fairway with a tail hook toward the green. I took my stance and waggled the club carefully, aware that image of the shot was incredibly vivid. Then I swung and the ball followed the path laid down in my mind."[8] A couple of holes later, the round turns bad for Murphy. Fearing a patch of gorse on the left side of the fairway, Murphy overcompensates and drives the ball far to the left into the hazard he tried to avoid, enacting the self-fulfilling prophecy of disaster that Parent describes. Regaining composure for Murphy begins with his gradual awareness of the power of visualization, and Shivas's coaxing to let go of his anxieties and control the ball not by mechanics but by imagination. "Now did ye e'er make a ball curve in the air just by willin' it?" Shivas asks.[9]

In a later part of *Golf in the Kingdom*, Murphy relates lessons gleaned from Shivas's notebooks, a collection of reminiscences and reflections like Penick's *Little Red Book* but with a stronger influence of Eastern mysticism and New Age philosophy. In one of his meditation exercises, Shivas instructs: "Imagine a golf ball. Make the image of it as vivid as you can. When anything intrudes upon the image, let it pass. If the golf ball disappears, imagine it again. If it wavers, make it steady. Doing this you can practice keeping your eye on the ball."[10] Exercises in visualization, Murphy says, have improved his play: "It is easer now to see the ball and the golf course as one unbroken field. . . . An image in our mind can become an irresistible path."[11] Murphy's experience demonstrates the lessons that Penick and Parent have offered as alternatives to the frustrating attempt to exert rigorous control over our game—the paradoxical *via negativa* of golf, which would have us imagine the golf ball out of existence in order to become more adept at hitting it.

14 HOW THE GOLF BALL LOOKS INTO THE ABYSS, AND THE ABYSS LOOKS BACK

In September 2000, before my wedding, my brother took me to Ireland. We flew into Dublin, rented a tiny silver car, and drove down to Kinsale, in County Cork, for a round at famous Old Head, a green drapery of links on the rock cliffs at the southernmost tip of the country. We spent our first night drinking at the Spaniard Inn in Kinsale, and we stayed the night in a foul hostel with clogged toilets. Already late for our early morning tee time, we woke with throbbing heads, stuffed our golf bags into the Lilliputian hatchback, and started for the course. We realized only later that we left our golf shoes in the hostel.

But as we crossed the isthmus leading to the wider headland, the bad funk of the cramped car, the hostel, and the hangover started to wash away. The morning was overcast and brisk but enlivened by a bracing ocean wind that shook the gorse and tufts of long grass. There were only a few other players on the course. We had the whole place to ourselves, and the bemused club pro was happy to lend some golf shoes to a couple of Yanks who had come so far to play the Head.

Buoyed, we took the first tee and commenced play of the two worst rounds the course had ever seen. Unfamiliar with links courses, we misjudged every distance and roll, found every bunker. The high winds ripped our drives left and right, out of bounds. Our heads ached and our spirits sank, until we simply surrendered and stopped keeping score.

We didn't enter some blessed emptiness that allowed us play better golf, as readers of *Golf in the Kingdom* might expect—we still couldn't hit a fairway. But something changed. The ache in our heads ebbed, pushed back by the beauty—all grass and mist and rock cliff and wind and sea. We hit our shots oblivious of strategy and thought, enjoying the strike of the club, the flight of the ball, regardless of its destination. We walked the back nine as if we were two primitives finding the land for the first time. On the footpath from the seventeenth green to the eighteenth tee, we stopped on the edge of a grassy precipice, where Ireland plunged hundreds of feet into the crashing waves. The mist in the air before us made the distance seem infinite. Here was what we came for. Here was the Head.

We emptied our pockets and our bags of all the balls we had left and scattered them in the long grass at the edge of the cliff. We drove them high and far into the mist over the ocean, where they disappeared into the white void. Our swings were perfect, our strikes pure, and the balls we hit seemed never to land. As I watched each one merge with the elements, I felt changed, like I was launching myself into nothingness. How could such a dull object as a golf ball transport me in that moment from hangover to ecstasy, from a Cork headland to the edge of the numinous?

In *Golf in the Kingdom*, when Murphy sends his ball down a rocky cliff and into the ocean, Shivas consoles him. "Ye try too hard and ye think too much. . . . Let the nothingness into your shots."[1] Like Harvey Penick and Joseph Parent, Shivas suggests that playing good golf depends not on the mastery of control but rather on giving up control. After Shivas opens Murphy to "the nothingness," Murphy becomes "more aware of the *feeling* of the game." His play improves and, more important, he learns a "lesson in resignation and simple sensing" of "the endless charms of Burningbush." "It was a new way to play for me," he says. "I had always been so focused on the score and the mechanics of the swing. . . . Now my focus of awareness included other things like the heather and the waves coming in from the sea."[2]

This surrender of control leads Murphy to a new sensory awareness, a total experience in which land, player, and ball merge into unity, as if "a presence was brooding through it all."[3] Later in the book, Murphy reflects on this "blending" of one's consciousness with the surrounding environment, the abandonment of self mediated by the golf ball. He includes a facsimile page from Shivas's notebooks:

Walking the course you can learn many things from your new found friends, the tree rooted deeply to he ground, firm, the upper branches swaying as natural as the breeze flowing through it. So reflect on your stance as you pass the tree. Can you do this, can you see the brook that golfers fear and not fearing but feeling can you put that flowing water into your swing? The green grass restful to body, soothing to soul. Is it so many paces that you put on it, or is it a period of rest and calmness between you and the ly of your ball. Be the tree rooted, be the brook flowing, be the calmness of the green.[4]

Joseph Parent's advice in *Zen Golf* has the same mystical tone: "give up control to get control." Play golf with your "intuitive mind," Parent writes, not with your "thinking mind."[5] You can't force a good shot, Parent says, any more that you can force a flower to open.[6]

This notion of higher consciousness attained by giving up conscious control of the ball and letting "the nothingness" into your shots represents a curious trend in the phenomenology of golf: transcendence through negation of the ball. As Shivas makes his epic approach to the elevated thirteenth green at Burningbush, the ball momentarily disappears as Murphy watches its flight over the vast patch of gorse called Lucifer's Rug. "When he swung I could not see the ball in flight," Murphy recalls. "I blinked as I looked up, but it had disappeared."[7] The ball reappears on the green, as if Shivas had willed it there. "Someday perhaps the ba' will na' come down again," Shivas says earlier in the round. "Have ye e'er had tha' feelin'?"[8] For my brother and me at Old Head, the balls that we hit into the white void never did come down.

Seeing the ball as "a nothingness," a disappearing signifier, turns it into a semiotic black hole, a practically endless receptacle of meaning for golfers of imagination. For Murphy, the white golf ball recalls Herman Melville's white whale: "Its power as a symbol is so complex and labyrinthine, so capable of lending itself to the psyche of each and every player, that once an attempt like this has begun to comprehend its 'inner meaning,' all bearings may be lost."[9] For Melville, whiteness contains both life and death, "not so much a color as the visible absence of color, and at the same time the concrete of all colors . . . there is such a dumb blankness, full of meaning."[10] What horrifies Ishmael in *Moby-Dick* fascinates Murphy. Whiteness, at once all colors and no color, seems talismanic in its ability to contain multiple and contradicting meanings.

In his final meditation on the ball, Murphy's imagination trips between whiteness and blackness, everything and nothing, finding one inside the other in one looping vision. He ponders a golf ball painted black, as if to mark a puncture in the curtain of reality and reveal the black empty space behind it: "Emptiness within emptiness."[11] The image of the ball as a nothingness reminds Murphy of another one of Shivas's photographic experiments. In the image, the ball, flying toward the camera, hangs frozen in the air only a few feet from the lens, eclipsing the sun as it fills the camera eye with its blackness. "A black ball, coming with terrific velocity!" Murphy recalls. The memory of the image returns to him like a premonition of death, a Satanic moon blocking the light of the sun or an obsidian meteor falling to Earth. "Sometimes when I am falling asleep the memory of it brings me awake with a start."[12] At Old Head, the experience of watching golf balls merge with the void deeply impressed me, not as a nightmare from the abyss but rather as a dream of flight, as if the ball were a projection of myself that I could ride to eternity.

15 HOW THE GOLF BALL WON THE GOLDEN FLEECE

In 1552, the town of St. Andrews set aside a tract for the "rearing of rabbits" and the "playing of golf." As such the first golf course was conceived as a kind of wildlife preserve and public park, exempt from the plow and open to all visitors.[1] Robert Browning explains that the original arrangement of eighteen holes, now standard in the game, was "purely arbitrary . . . and accidental" at St. Andrews. On early links courses, the number and layout of the holes was determined by the layout of the ground, with two loops—one "out" and the other "home." While modern courses are intentionally constructed to pose particular strategic challenges, the "cross country game" of the old courses compelled players "to take the links as they found it."[2]

In his investigation of the historical origins of the game, Browning distinguishes the basic elements of golf from those of "kindred games" like hockey and pall-mall, or the medieval

Dutch games *chole* and *kolven*. "The idea of hitting a ball with a crooked stick," he writes, "is so primitive as to be common to all countries. Yet the simple fact remains that it was the Scots who devised the essential features of golf, the *combination* of hitting for distance with the final nicety of approach to an exiguous mark, and the independent progress of each player with his own ball, free from interference by his adversary."[3] In this sense, we define golf as an individual endeavor, each player possessing and controlling his own ball—a kind of cross-country solitaire, unique in its conception of gameplay as an odyssey in microcosm, the ball a tiny but swift vessel in flight over hazards to green islands of safety.[4] In this archetypal conception of the game, the ball is not a medium for competition between two or more players, as it is in other games, but rather a medium for navigation between player and field, a means for expanding one's reach and range of movement across a landscape, a satellite of oneself.

On early links courses, without a designer imposing a theory on the landscape, players themselves "designed" the best path to the green. Influenced by this notion of golf as a cross-country trek, Alister MacKenzie scorns the "card and pencil" players of modern courses who shoot merely to score and lack the "spirit of adventure" of crossing exciting terrain.[5] A. W. Tillinghast, another designer of MacKenzie's era, envisioned the building of new golf courses as the opening of new country, an expression of the same expansionist impulse that drove pioneers into wild country to build roads and farms.[6] MacKenzie also envisioned the game as a journey of discovery. "There is charm," he writes, "in exploring fresh country" during a round of golf.[7] We find this idea of golf as an imaginative journey expressed not only in the reflections of these pioneering golf course architects but also in the vernacular tributes attached to special holes and hazards that have become official monikers, named after the remote and sublime places of the earth: the "Sahara" and the "Alps" on the seventeenth at Prestwick, the "Himalayas" on the sixth at St. Enodoc, and the "Eden" on the eleventh at St. Andrews.

At the dinner party hosted by Adam and Eve Greene in *Golf in the Kingdom*, Shivas Irons quotes his ancient teacher Seamus MacDuff, for whom golf is an "odyssey from world to world. . . . from hole to hole, adventure after adventure, comic and tragic, spellin' out the human drama. . . . In all o' that 'tis a microcosm of the world, a good stage for the drama of self-discovery."[8] For Shivas, the notion of a "round" has metaphysical implications: "it leads back to the place you started from." Because most courses are constructed in a way that situates the last green near the first tee, Shivas's observation is more than allegorical. Indeed, as Shivas says, "golf is always a trip back to the first tee." Murphy feels this sense of death and rebirth even more acutely at Burningbush, where the eighteenth green, according to local memory, was built on the grave of some forgotten shepherd or crofter.[9]

Adam describes golf not merely as a life's journey writ small but also as a "recapitulation" of the evolution of the human species. He traces the essential pleasure of seeing a ball in flight to our "Paleolithic past, from the hunt." Like a spear or a stone flying toward a quarry, the ball in flight stirs our memory of the hunt, but it also "anticipates our desire for transcendence." He describes hitting the sweet spot as a "Promethean" experience and regards technological advances in clubs and balls like the gift of fire, bestowing on humanity "new powers and awareness." Adam offers a different perspective on the material evolution of the ball, which he views not merely as a commodity born of the imperial rubber trade or postwar plastics research, nor even as a threat to standards of competition and course construction, but rather as a vehicle capable of lifting a golfer's psyche higher and farther—spiritual transcendence via gutta-percha and synthetic polymers. "The thrill of seeing a ball fly over the countryside, over obstacles—especially over a stretch of water—and then onto the green and into the hole has a mystic quality," Adam decides at last. "Something in us *loves* that flight."[10]

While old courses like St. Andrews, St. Enodoc, and Prestwick continue to embody the origin of golf as a cross-country trek, more recent courses, designed by architects who share Murphy's vision of golf as a symbolic migration of body and mind, attempt to externalize imaginary odysseys with high-concept designs. At Stone Harbor Golf Club in New Jersey, Desmond Muirhead conceives each hole as an episode from Greek mythology. The par-3 seventh represents the quest of Jason and the Argonauts, who sailed between perilous cliffs called the Clashing Rocks to claim the Golden Fleece. The hole featured an island green shaped like a boat, flanked on each side by two island bunkers shaped like jagged rocks. Players found the design both outlandish and intimidating, and the club reconstructed the hole in a more traditional form shortly after its construction. At Shadow Creek in Nevada, Tom Fazio found inspiration not in Greek myth but in Hollywood magic. Conjured out of a barren desert, the course resembles a gigantic movie set, with fiberglass boulders, an artificial stream and waterfall, and one hole designed to evoke the drama of walking into a sports arena, with a huge circular berm carpeted with thousands of flowers. "Everything's an illusion" at Shadow Creek, the golf architect Bob Cupp says.[11]

Both Fazio and Muirhead construct a landscape the way a writer tells a story, modulating emotional response with features designed to evoke in the player feelings of anticipation, struggle, and rapturous resolution—the completion of a quest, the end of a journey. If the ball, as Shivas Irons describes it, is an "egg" from which we might emerge in the course of play, the hole is our final destination, our return to the earth, our Golden Fleece.[12]

16 HOW THE GOLF BALL WENT TO THE MOON

Two hours before dawn on January 31, 1971, Alan Shepard, Stuart Roosa, and Edgar Mitchell sat in their capsule on top of the massive Saturn V rocket, awaiting the launch of Apollo 14. What does a person think about in the moments before leaving one world and going to another? Maybe Shepard was thinking about James Lovell, commander of the aborted and nearly fatal Apollo 13 mission, which had preceded them less than a year earlier. *Would they make it to the moon?* Maybe he was thinking about Gus Grissom, one of the original Mercury astronauts like Shepard himself, who burned to death with Edward White and Roger Chaffee in their Apollo 1 capsule during a mission rehearsal. *Would he make it off the launch pad?* Or maybe, in some corner of his mind, Shepard was thinking about Bob Hope, who had given him the madcap notion, during a tour of the NASA complex a few years earlier, to whack a golf ball on the moon.

Would he make it five hundred yards—a thousand—in that long hitter's gravity?

He would see. Stuffed into his white sock, beneath his suit, known only to a few mission planners, he had two golf balls and the head of a six iron, which he would attach to retractable shovel handle. Shepard had been the second man in space back in 1961, just after the Russian, Yuri Gagarin. Now, at the farthest frontier of human exploration, in the Fra Mauro Hills, near the Sea of Rains, he would hit a golf ball.

He had practiced. Some days, after the usual astronaut training, he climbed into a pressure suit and hit balls in some side lot with one arm, as the stiff and bulky suit would allow. He knew his shot would be televised, recorded, and celebrated in the annals of both the space program and the game. He could not look like a stooge, duffing his shot, or worse, falling over backwards with the momentum of his own wild swing. He must have *seen* the shot, as Harvey Penick or Joseph Parent would have instructed. He must have seen the tangerine sky of the Texas afternoon turn vacuum black, the green turf turn to gray-white powder. He could hit his six-iron 150 yards or more at River Oaks Country Club in Houston. Could he loft it to that crater 900 yards away? Farther? What does one think about in the moments before hitting a golf ball on the moon? *I will hit it farther than anyone has ever hit it. I will go farther than anyone has ever gone.*

"In my left hand, I have a little white pellet that's familiar to millions of Americans," Shepard quips to the camera, near the end of the second and last extravehicular activity (EVA) of the Apollo 14 mission, in the moon's Fra Mauro Hills. Shepard plops two golf balls into the lunar dust, squares his stance, and takes a firm, one-armed swing, as he practiced. He misses.

Standing near Shepard, Ed Mitchell says, "You got more dirt than ball that time."

Shepard swings again, knocking the ball only a few feet to his right. "That looked like a slice to me, Al," Mitchell, says.

Undaunted, Shepard resets for his third try. "Here we go," he says. "Straight as a die. One more."

This time he connects. As we watch the shot through the eye of the television camera that the crew set up to record the EVA, the ball flies off to the right. He squares to the second ball, swings, and connects, sending it, too, off into the distance. "Miles and miles and miles."[1]

When Shepard came back, he gave the improvised six-iron, the "moon club," to the USGA Museum in Far Hills, New Jersey, where you can see it now. He also gave the museum his socks, where he stowed the balls on board the spacecraft. The golf balls themselves are still up there, somewhere in the Fra Mauro Hills, maybe 300 yards from the Apollo 14 landing site. A mission photograph shows one of them resting in a small crater, a clean lie, near a "javelin," a small metal bar hurled by Ed Mitchell. The two objects had been cast into the crater partly to demonstrate for the television audience the low lunar gravity, and partly just for fun—happy indulgences by men on the moon who, for a brief moment before climbing back into the ascent module and leaving forever, became boys on a playground.

Why has Shepard's golf shot become iconic, an indelible image in our cultural memory, while Mitchell's javelin throw has been forgotten? In the mission photograph, the two forlorn objects rest there in the dust, side by side, both monuments to the human ingenuity it took to get there and the primordial pleasure of hurling an object against heaven. But only the ball has that weird aura of an object out of place, out of rational context, like a Photoshopped hoax picture. The javelin looks merely like a discarded tool. It could easily be a hammer or a stray piece of rebar at an abandoned work site. But that ball. What's it doing there on the moon? What does it mean that Shepard left it there?

Along with the star-spangled banner planted in the Sea of Tranquility by Neil Armstrong seven months prior to Apollo 14, Shepard's golf ball represents one of the first claims of culture upon a truly precultural, unhuman landscape. Like Armstrong's flag, Shepard's golf ball signals an act of possession, but Shepard did not mark the moon as colonized territory, as Armstrong did. Instead, he seemed to claim it as a new pleasure ground. Smuggling the golf balls and the six-iron in his sock, Shepard acted unofficially, even irresponsibly, in pure fancy. That golf ball in the lunar dust, in contrast to the flag, seems to open the possibility that this new world might become something other than a military outpost or science research station. The moon—space itself—could become a new field of play, where we might project our dreams miles and miles and miles.

In *Golf in the Kingdom*, Shivas Irons, like Alan Shepard, seems mesmerized by the image of a golf ball in space. He ponders the "ubiquity" of the ball in flight. As a global game, golf is always being played somewhere, on one of the planet's 35,000 golf courses. The ball "is in flight at this very moment," Shivas reflects, "above every continent. Moreover, it is in flight every moment of the day and night. . . . Consider the symbolism inherent in that indubitable fact: a golf ball suspended in air at every moment!"[2] Murphy thinks of the ball as a kind of "satellite," permanently flying above the earth.

Imagining the ball as a "satellite," Murphy considers the significance of Shepard's improvised six-iron shot on the moon, an event that strikes him as both historical and metaphysical. He marvels that golf has become "the first human game played on another planetary body" and takes the event as proof that "the game has a mighty destiny."[3] The ubiquitous golf ball, "the little white pellet that's familiar to millions of Americans," as Shepard says, becomes, at that moment, a vehicle not only for a trek across terrestrial landscapes but also for humanity's expansion into the cosmos.

Lunar explorers have left a lot of litter on the moon, most of it the detritus of exploration itself: landing vehicles, rovers, crashed orbiters, television cameras, hammers and sundry tools, and plastic bags for astronaut feces. These objects were not meant to say anything. Some had played their part in the journey and had become useless. Some had been dumped to make room for other objects, moon rocks, on the return journey. None of them were meant to say anything.

Other objects shot into space were meant to say a lot. *Fallen Astronaut*, a memorial sculpture created by Paul Van Hoeydonck and left on the moon by the crew of Apollo 15 in August 1971, commemorates all the men up to that time who died in the quest to explore space. The Golden Record on board the Voyager probes contains musical selections, images, and voice recordings intended by mission planners to serve as an abridged version of human scientific and cultural achievement, a message in a bottle for unknown alien correspondents. A DVD, now on board the abandoned Phoenix lander near the Martian north pole, declared its intention to speak to future human colonists of Mars, with works of science fiction reflecting our hopes and fears about what the red planet holds in store for us.

As Shepard himself must have sensed hitting golf balls on the moon, as I sensed hitting golf balls on the cliffs at Old Head, we identify ourselves by the objects we cast into the void. We drop a coin into a wishing well, a good faith payment to fate. We seal photographs, letters, and artifacts in a time capsule and bury it in the earth for a distant posterity. We send a message in a bottle, hoping to find some chink in the insurmountable bastion of solitude. We fling into space for some unknown entities inscribed disks that signify our essence.

Alan Shepard's golf ball was unique. It served neither a mission objective nor the human vanity in declaring our achievement to the universe. It was something like a joke, a toy. His six-iron shot in the Fra Mauro Hills, which came to a clean lie in a nearby crater, suggests an attempt to take possession of a wild landscape by playing with it, an extension of the human will and human folly in the wildest of places.

17 HOW THE GOLF BALL MAKES FRIENDS WITH ANIMALS

The casual golfer really has no need to buy new golf balls. On every golf course in the world they lay scattered profusely in the weeds, the woods, and water, more plentiful and available than crabapples, just at the edge of a casual glance. Even a minimal effort at searching the fringes of the course will fill your pockets. One hot day last year, my cart parked by a wire fence separating the eighteenth fairway from a neighboring pasture, I found ten balls within as many feet of the cart, though I never found the ball I hit into the weeds on that fence line. I suppose that many more balls lay within the short radius of my search, and perhaps hundreds of others along that whole fence: one undiscovered constellation within a vast galaxy of lost balls.

The notorious par-3 seventeenth hole at TPC Sawgrass in Florida is the Bermuda Triangle of golf. According to the estimate of club officials, players plop more than 120,000 balls a year into the water surrounding its island green—almost 330 daily, and about three per each foursome of golfers who play the hole. Companies that sell "pre-owned" balls pay a recovery fee to send divers into the shallow pond to salvage the balls. With these salvage divers making between $50,000 to $100,000 a year recovering balls from Sawgrass and other courses in south Florida, some consider these hazards the "most lucrative waters in the entire golf ball business." Golf Balls Galore sells two million balls a year recovered from Florida courses alone.[1] Lostgolfballs.com offers the top brands—Titleist, Callaway, Bridgestone, Srixon, Nike, TaylorMade, and Volvik—at a steep discount. In 2010, Gary Shienfeld of Knetgolf estimated that he sold twenty million recovered golf balls, reaping much of his profit from burgeoning golf markets in China, India, and Southeast Asia.[2]

The big business of recovering, restoring, repackaging, and shipping lost golf balls to Beijing or Singapore begins with one guy wading into the muck, sometimes in diving gear, sometimes with nothing more than a mesh bag and his bare hands. Sometimes they have a retractable grabber, a specialized tool designed for snatching golf balls out of precarious places. In an essay on lost golf balls, John McPhee relates his own purchase of the Orange Trapper, a modest nine-foot grabber that he uses to pluck balls from the stony bed of the Delaware River or pilfer them from inside the fences of Princeton golf clubs. McPhee hasn't played golf in sixty years, he explains; the Orange Trapper serves only to satisfy his compulsion to collect lost balls, which he donates to First Tee, a youth golf program. Use of the Orange Trapper requires patience and concentration, even skill. McPhee compares it to his fly rod and perfects a technique for using it in a moving canoe.[3]

The market offers other ball recovery contraptions, more technically sophisticated, if not more elegant, than McPhee's Orange Trapper. You can buy special glasses fitted with lenses that filter out colored light, making a white golf ball nestled in high grass or tangled underbrush appear to glow. The Findable Golf Ball System uses a radar beam that interacts with a tag embedded in a golf ball, beeping with increasing frequency, like a homing device in a spy movie, as you approach your concealed target. If price is no concern, and you don't want to risk the two-stroke penalty on outdated tech like radar or light-filtering lenses, you can try the Ball Finder Scout—a digital eye that locates lost balls with high-resolution photography and pixel analysis.

But what happens to all those balls that don't get recovered by salvage divers, Orange Trappers, radar guns, or digital spy cameras? John Updike finds poetry in these lost objects. In the foreword of Charles Lindsay's *Lost Balls*, a photographic collection of "great holes, tough shots, and bad lies," Updike writes: "For every lost ball there was a forlorn search, perfunctory or thorough; these questing ghosts haunt the course, hovering at the juncture of their interrupted game. 'Found it!' one wants to cry out in triumph, though the loser has been decades in his grave."[4]

Lindsay himself is equally pensive. "Every lost ball," he says, "was once a shot of hope and aspiration that then became a plop in the water." For Updike and Lindsay, the lost ball is an accidental memento mori, a reminder that the greatest of golf legends shares the fate of the most hopeless hacker. Lindsay reserves a special place in *Lost Balls* for the 2003 Open Championship at Royal St. George's in Kent, when Tiger Woods lost his drive from the first tee, incurred a two-stroke penalty, and eventually lost the tournament by two strokes. "The golf shot," Lindsay writes in his Afterword, "with its aspiration, trajectory, and distance, seems to mirror human ambition, to take measure of our successes and failures." The lost ball seems to remind us of the folly of our ambition, the final sum of our successes and failures.[5]

While lost balls compel Updike and Lindsay to ponder mortality, they can also draw us beyond the safe and familiar boundaries of our experience and bring us into contact with another, secret life. Our vision becomes more minutely attuned to the environment through the search for a lost ball. To find it, we must adjust our perspective to the ball's scale and see the world as the ball sees it. Updike becomes mesmerized as the golf ball draws him into a world that normally escapes our attention:

Tangles of running raspberry, shadowy depths of a deep sand bunker, sandy beds of shallow little watercress-choked creeks, weedy lees of lichen-laden stone walls, snake-infested moonscapes of pre-Cambrian basalt just off the plush watered fairways of a desert course, the pulpy flesh of a venerable saguaro cactus, the leaf-mulched floor of a hushed beech forest, the squishy hummocks of a reedy marsh.[6]

When we are in these places with the ball, Updike thinks, we interact with the landscape at a "visceral level." Our vision is transformed. We might become a worm in examining the lie of a ball nested in "pebbles and tufts," or a hawk in seeking the "telltale glint" of a ball in a "wide, wind-whitened world of rough." He seems to stretch the limits of language in an effort to describe an alien and arresting experience of nature suddenly opened to us by the loss of a golf ball. Lindsay echoes Updike's sense of enchanted displacement in his Afterword. He writes that he has learned to "celebrate" the errant shot because it draws him out of himself: "Gigantic hooks and pushes take me into ankle-deep muck, far from the fairway, fighting the sagebrush, dodging the poison ivy, and looking for a white orb as round as the moon."[7]

Lindsay's joy at being diverted into the muck and the sagebrush may account for the many images in Lost Balls showing the potential for golf balls to lure people into encounters with animals that might otherwise remain invisible or ignored. In this way, he illustrates Updike's idea that the golf ball, especially when lost, can mediate new encounters with the natural world. A diver plucking balls from Florida ponds might meet cottonmouths, snapping turtles, and alligators competing for the salvage rights. A grizzly bear might lumber out of the underbrush at the edge of the green at the Yellowstone Club in Montana. We recall the episode of *Seinfeld* that had George Costanza uncorking the blowhole of a beached whale, finding there a Titleist that Kramer had driven from the shore—"a hole in one!" At Carne Golf Links in County Mayo, Ireland, a player gets a free drop if a fox or a raven snatches a ball. The club Secretary, James O'Hara, estimates that the ravens once stole seventy-two balls on a single day.

These comic and occasionally dangerous scenes demonstrate the tendency of errant golf balls to find the boundary between domesticated and wild landscapes. In one of the most striking photographs in Lindsay's collection, a disfigured ball lies abandoned in the daisies at Carne; a fox has chewed and shredded its white cover, revealing the yellow-orange polyurethane core beneath. With its skin flayed like petals and the bright disk at its core, the ball itself has bloomed like a mutated daisy, popping out of the flowery grass. In another image, a cluster of golf balls is visible in a clump of bear scat, along with berries, pine needles, and other partially digested material.

Narrowing his focus to the "worm's-eye view" described by Updike, Lindsay includes other images that seem alien in the way they open a window to a microscopic scale, where the golf ball is transformed from a small white pellet to a massive spheroid. Two amber snails explore the surface of a Raw Distance 408dr Titanium lost in the rough at Old Head (perhaps one of the balls clubbed out of bounds by my brother or me). A swarm of fire ants covers a ball that has impacted their nest in a bunker at the Old Marsh Golf Club in Palm Beach, as if trying to devour or assimilate the threat to their colony. McPhee observes a similar phenomenon canoeing on the Delaware, where lampreys slithering among the rocks on the bottom have integrated lost golf balls into the construction of their nests, built from stones shoved into circular fortresses that remind McPhee of the "craters of the moon."[8] Lindsay documents that red-tailed hawks nesting at Bethpage also like to use golf balls to line their nests, or else collect them as simulacra of their eggs.

The difference between the organic and the inorganic seems to dissolve in one more image of a small clan of ladybugs who have found an accommodating nest in a gutta-percha ball marked with brambles and widely split at the center. The ball is more than a century old, and the person who last played it lies in his grave. Resting in peace in among dried weeds and twigs, its shell split and its interior brown and dank like humus, the old guttie could be some fungal puffball disgorging its trillion spores, except for the regularly formed pattern on its surface, imprinted there in a *fin-de-siècle* rubber factory. The manufactured object has at last been degraded and absorbed, the ladybugs going in and digging out their space, the acids of the soil slowly turning the surface brown. The earth itself ushers the golf ball to the next stage of its evolution, changing it from an industrial object existing in historical time to an organic object existing in biological and geographic time.

18 HOW THE GOLF BALL PREPARES FOR DOOMSDAY

Once upon a time my dad owned dogs, and he used to walk them in fields along a country road near our house. Sometimes he would practice his iron play in those empty fields, releasing the dogs to chase the balls.

Now the dogs are gone, and the fields are planted with tidy new residential developments. During the few years he watched those houses pop up on his private sporting reserve, he indulged a compulsion to leave a hidden signature, a territorial marker. In the long evenings between late spring and early autumn, when the construction crews had left and he went to the fields with his dogs, a nine iron, and a pocket full of balls, he would approach a building site and press golf balls deep into the wet concrete of the new foundation, so that they will be encased there as long as the house stands. If the concrete was already dry, he would drop a ball or two into the dark recess of a cinderblock or slip it into a nook under the lumber of a raw floor.

He mentions this compulsion to me whenever we pass those houses, now occupied by people who walk their own dogs and plant gardens and park SUVs in those lots. He tells me proudly that he has left the golf balls in the framework of their homes, that they'll never know—that no one will ever know—until those houses fall down, and all the houses built on top of them fall down, and some future archaeologist excavates the land and finds an ancient, crumbling foundation embedded with a white, dimpled polyurethane orb. *A ball for golf, yes, a game they played,* this archaeologist of the future might say, *but what's it doing here in this concrete? Surely it wasn't part of the construction. Was it ritual—some means of consecrating the house? Was it merely accident?*

I don't think the archaeologist could know, because I don't think my dad knew. Was it ritual, a way of holding his ground in that field as others came to stake their claim? A blessing on the house, or a curse? It was, at least, no accident. A human hand put the ball into the concrete, but what would remove it, and when? My dad likes to wonder about these things when he drives by the fields where he used to walk his dogs and hit nine-iron shots, and where now stand pink and yellow houses with SUVs in the driveway. He likes to think that when all this is gone, crumbled into dust, those golf balls will be there—*he* will be there.

Like my dad, John Updike and Charles Lindsay sense in lost and decomposing golf balls the beginning of some unknown archaeology of the future. Updike writes that golf leaves a "residue, thin but detectable."[1] The first layers of this residue are already visible in our own time, taking us back to the earlier stages in the evolution of the golf ball. Lindsay photographs a "Pluto" gutta-percha ball from 1905, half buried in the earth at the Myopia Hunt Club in Massachusetts, with black dimples showing through a coat of white paint. A close-up of another half-buried ball takes us back even further toward the game's origins: a gutta-percha ball from the late nineteenth century, its surface cut and scarred by antique irons, in the dunes of St. Andrews.

One of the final images in *Lost Balls* is, as Lindsay explains, "possibly the world's oldest golf ball," made of boxwood with an iron core, excavated from an early sixteenth-century trash heap, lost, perhaps in the reign of Henry VIII; a wooden club head found nearby dates to 1432. The person who wielded the club cursed his slice in the Middle English of Chaucer's *Canterbury Tales*. The images of these burnished wooden artifacts in a book mostly about the modern game seem as odd as the image, also included in the book, of a modern ball that has rolled out of bounds and come to rest in the ruins of the fourteenth-century castle at the Pennard Golf Club in Swansea. In both images, Lindsay collapses time around the ball. It seems simultaneously ancient and modern, incarnate in lathed boxwood in a twenty-first-century museum, and in a polyurethane pill in a medieval stone tower. Lindsay muses on the ways future archaeologists and cultural historians might interpret the "curious language" on the Victorian golf balls that he has found and photographed: *Pluto, Bambi, Long and Straight, Wanker, Revelation*. Both Lindsay and my father imagine these many lost golf balls as a "future stratigraphy, the detritus of wishful players' misplaced hopes."[2] Might some Wanker ride his shot Long and Straight toward Revelation?

The salvage divers who snag submerged balls while dodging cottonmouths, snapping turtles, and gators recall some other detritus they have found in the muddy substrate of Florida's manicured landscapes, slowly compacting into this future stratigraphy: golf clubs, of course, and golf bags with wallets—identities—still inside. Golf carts, too, and handguns, and a Barbie doll, and a telephone booth, and a Volkswagen with the driver (what's left) still at the wheel.[3] What will these future archaeologists say about us and our diversions, our toys and our games, our guns and our cars? Will they understand us better than we understand ourselves?

In a chorus from his play, *The Rock*, T. S. Eliot writes:

In the land of lobelias and tennis flannels
The rabbit shall burrow and the thorn revisit,
The nettle shall flourish on the gravel court,
And the wind shall say: "Here were a decent
    and godless people:
The only monument the asphalt road
And a thousand lost golf balls."[4]

The critic Hugh Kenner interprets the golf ball in Eliot's play as the distillation of all the accumulated banalities of modernity. For Eliot, Kenner suggests, the pocked sphere is "an object of nearly ideal triviality," a perfect emblem of "people lacking myths." Their existence devoid of meaning, such a civilization is "given over to obsessive patterns of action they have no way to justify," empty imitations of ritual, like golf. Kenner wryly observes, "I find it interesting that no novel of pretension occupies itself with golf; something there is about the golf ball that does not love myth."[5]

We might call John McPhee's compulsive collection of balls, or my dad's compulsive burial of them, "obsessive patterns of action"—personal rituals adopted in old age. Both men find it difficult to "justify" or explain these rituals, but they are not devoid of myth, at least personal ones. Both men invest the balls with a measure of themselves. Both have a consciousness of the ball's endurance on a time scale that exceeds their own. For both, the object, the ritual, becomes a way to persist in time, McPhee creating his legacy by donating his recovered balls to charity and my dad by leaving his time capsules in concrete foundations.

Maybe not even the author of *The Waste Land* could have imagined a scene surreal as a remote submersible crawling the bottom of Loch Ness in search of a prehistoric reptile and finding instead a thousand lost golf balls, or rather a hundred thousand, with perhaps even a thousand thousand in the unexplored abyssal blackness beyond lights and sonar.

In 2009 a search for the Loch Ness monster revealed more than 100,000 balls on the floor of the loch. Bafflement among researchers soon gave way to the realization that local golfers have been using the Loch Ness as a picturesque driving range, perhaps for centuries.

The image of 100,000 lost balls scattered in the monster's deep domain attracted worldwide attention to the potential environmental problem posed by the millions of other balls submerged in lakes, rivers, and marshes in all the other golfing countries of the world. Patrick Harvie, a local government minister at Loch Ness, declared: "From the moon to Loch Ness, golf balls are humanity's signature litter in the most inaccessible locations."[6] His indictment prompted inevitable speculations about the litter we cast into these inaccessible locations. How many balls do we lose? What happens to them in their invisible afterlife?

If we extrapolate the estimates of greenskeepers and club professionals at TPC Sawgrass and many other courses, the current best guess is that 300 million golf balls are lost in the United States each year.[7] If we further extrapolate the findings of ecologists who study the environmental impact of golf—that about half of the golf played on Earth is played in the United States—then we can roughly estimate that 600 million golf balls get lost on the planet each year.[8] If we then factor all the salvage divers, Orange Trappers, sunglasses that make golf balls glow, golf ball radar, golf ball spy cameras, and all the companies recovering and selling used golf balls, we might also say, for the sake of discussion, that roughly 100 million lost balls are recovered, leaving about half a billion balls lost each year in all the "inaccessible locations" of the planet.

Here we venture past the limits of technical knowledge. No one has studied what happens to these lost balls. No one knows how long it takes a golf ball to decompose; estimates range from a hundred years to a thousand years. No one knows whether this accumulating stratum of billions of lost golf balls poses an environmental hazard. Danish researchers have observed that "dangerous levels of zinc" in decomposing golf balls can poison ecosystems and advocate the use of biodegradable golf balls. Others say that the environmental threat posed by lost golf balls, even millions of them, is negligible: five bottles of mouthwash contain more zinc than a million golf balls.[9]

Our most reliable source on the question might be Anthony Andrady, a polymer scientist whose study, *Plastics in the Environment*, has become an "oracle" on the ecological impact of plastics, according to Alan Weisman, author of *The World Without Us*. The problem, Andrady observes, is that many polymers, including those in golf balls, have been engineered for toughness, for resistance to biodegradation and photodegradation.[10] Although many plastics photodegrade faster than they biodegrade, they can last much longer in places shielded from heat and sunlight. Exposed to direct ultraviolet radiation and extreme temperatures, Shepard's moon balls might have already decomposed, but the many millions of balls submerged in the water and mud and sand and soil of the home planet rest in chthonic slumber, probably destined to outlast the race that made them. "Except for a small amount that's been incinerated," Andrady says, "every bit of plastic manufactured in the world from the last 50 years or so still remains. It's somewhere in the environment."[11] Microbes still haven't evolved the enzymes able to degrade plastic, so golf balls and other such artifacts linger, waiting for the environment to learn what to do with them. "No plastic has died a natural death yet," Andrady says. "But give it 100,000 years." Some opportunistic bug, perhaps, will learn how to eat a golf ball. If not, Andrady speculates, the Earth itself will eat them: "should biologic time run out and some plastics remain, there is always geologic time. The upheavals and pressure will change it into something else. Just like trees buried in bogs a long time ago—the geologic process, not biodegradation, changed them into oil and coal. Maybe high concentrations of plastics will turn into something like that."[12]

As Timothy Morton writes in *Hyperobjects*, ecology tells us that there are really no "u-bends" in the environment like those in our plumbing, no existential threshold beyond which we can send our waste to some "ontologically alien realm" where we need not think about it.[13] Whether our golf balls and Styrofoam cups and shopping bags get flushed into the ocean or buried underground, they become part of the geological record of our lives at the outset of the Anthropocene, the era marked by the human terraforming of the earth's landmass and atmosphere through global processes of manufacturing, consumption, and waste. In this sense, golf balls are indeed, as Eliot, Updike, Lindsay, and my dad envision, part of the archaeological record of modernity.

As we speculate about these posthuman time scales, we can make a few more amusing calculations. If we use a median estimate for the natural life span of a golf ball—500 years—and recall that some 500 million golf balls are lost each year, we can project that the planet will harbor in its infinite dark recesses about 250 billion lost golf balls five centuries from now, none of them having died a "natural death." Lined up in a chain, 250 billion balls of regulation length (42.67 mm) would measure about 10.7 million kilometers, roughly eight times the diameter of the sun and 28 times the distance from the Earth to the moon. A beam of light would take almost 36 seconds to travel from one end of the chain to the other. The volume of the same 250 million lost golf balls that will accumulate on the Earth in the next 500 years will be about 102 billion cubic meters, more than the volume of rock disgorged by Mount Tambora in Indonesia in 1815, the largest volcanic eruption on record.

We probably won't be playing golf (as we know it) in five centuries or even in one century. Maybe all balls will be biodegradable and the substrate of undecomposed polyurethane pellets will stand as a remnant of the unenlightened Plastic Age. Maybe our culture, chastened by some future environmental catastrophe, will reach the same decision about incorruptible polymers that Xi did about the Coke bottle: "The thing does not belong on the earth." Maybe the game, and golf balls themselves, will be entirely virtual while real golf excursions into the elemental realms of earth and air become increasingly expensive. However the game evolves, however we evolve, all those balls in Loch Ness, in the Florida swamps, and in the churning sea off the cliffs of Cork remain an indelible sign of the onset of the Anthropocene era: an object lesson from the moment in historical and geologic time when the human species liked to play games with nature but had not yet grasped all the rules.

NOTES

Chapter 1

1 *The Gods Must Be Crazy*, directed by Jamie Uys (Twentieth Century Fox, 1980).

2 T. S. Eliot, *The Rock*, quoted in Hugh Kenner, *Historical Fictions* (San Francisco: North Point Press, 1990), 85.

3 Timothy Morton, *Hyperobjects: Philosophy and Ecology after the End of the World* (Minneapolis: University of Minnesota Press, 2013), 36, 55.

Chapter 2

1 Michael Murphy, *Golf in the Kingdom* (New York: Arkana, 1972), 55.

2 Robert Browning, *A History of Golf: The Royal and Ancient Game* (London: A & W Black, 1990), 30.

3 Murphy, *Golf in the Kingdom*, 48.

4 Browning, *A History of Golf*, 135–6.

5 Browning, *A History of Golf*, 136.

6 Browning, *A History of Golf*, 137.

7 Browning, *A History of Golf*, 138.

8 Browning, *A History of Golf*, 137.

9 Browning, *A History of Golf*, 140.

Chapter 3

1 John Tully, "A Victorian Ecological Disaster: Imperialism, the Telegraph, and Gutta-Percha," *Journal of World History* 20 (2009): 559.

2 Browning, *A History of Golf*, 140.

3 "Golf Ball Inventor Dead," *New York Times*, April 26, 1904, accessed July 24, 2013, http://query.nytimes.com/mem/archive-free/pdf?_r=1&res=9C02E4DA1E3BE631A25755C2A9629C946597D6CF.

4 Browning, *A History of Golf*, 141.

5 Browning, *A History of Golf*, 141.

6 Browning, *A History of Golf*, 142.

7 "Conforming Golf Ball List," United States Golf Association, accessed July 24, 2013, https://www.usga.org/ConformingGolfBall/conforming_golf_ball.asp.

Chapter 4

1 John Updike, "The Big Bad Boom," in *Golf Dreams* (New York: Fawcett Columbine, 1996), 15.

2 Updike, "The Big Bad Boom," 116.

3 Updike, "The Big Bad Boom," 117.

4 Updike, "The Big Bad Boom," 119.

5 Richard J. Moss, *The Kingdom of Golf in America* (Lincoln: University of Nebraska Press, 2013), 50.

6 Moss, *The Kingdom of Golf in America*, 51.

7 Moss, *The Kingdom of Golf in America*, 52.

8 "Club Membership History," United States Golf Association, accessed February 5, 2015, http://www.usga.org/clubs_courses/club_history/Club-Membership/.

9 "By the Numbers: USA Golfers and Golf Courses," National Golf Foundation, accessed February 5, 2014, http://www.golf-info-guide.com/golf-tips/golf-in-the-usa/by-the-numbers-usa-golfers-and-golf-courses/.

10 John Lowerson, "Scottish Croquet: The English Golf Boom, 1880–1914," *History Today* 33 (1983), accessed February 5, 2014, http://www.historytoday.com/john-lowerson/scottish-croquet-english-golf-boom-1880-1914.

11 Osamu Saito, "Measuring the Lifecycle Carbon Footprint of a Golf Course and Greening the Golf Industry in Japan," (paper presented at the New Zealand Society for Sustainability Engineering and Science, November 30–December 3, 2010), http://www.thesustainabilitysociety.org.nz/conference/2010/papers/Saito.pdf.

12 Alister MacKenzie, *The Spirit of St. Andrews* (New York: Broadway Books, 1998), 41–2.

13 MacKenzie, *The Spirit of St. Andrews*, 83.

14 MacKenzie, *The Spirit of St. Andrews*, 44.

15 Tom Doak, *The Anatomy of a Golf Course: The Art of Golf Course Architecture* (Ithaca, NY: Burford Books, 1992), 71.

16 MacKenzie, *The Spirit of St. Andrews*, 67.

17 Mihaly Csikszentmihalyi, *Flow: The Psychology of Optimal Experience* (New York: Harper Perennial, 1991), 3.

18 Bobby Jones, *Golf Is My Game, 1961* (London: A & C Black, 1990), 20.

19 Csikszentmihalyi, *Flow*, 74–5.

20 Jones, *Golf Is My Game*, 202.

21 Jones, *Golf Is My Game*, 238.

22 Jones, *Golf Is My Game*, 238.

23 "2014 Stats," The Masters, accessed July 16, 2014, http://www.masters.com/en_US/scores/stats/index.html.

24 Bill Pennington, "In a Hole, Golf Considers Digging a Wider One," *New York Times*, accessed April 19, 2014, http://www.nytimes.com/2014/04/19/sports/golf/in-a-hole-golf-considers-digging-a-wider-one.html.

25 Pennington, "In a Hole, Golf Considers Digging a Wider One."

26 HackGolf, accessed July 16, 2014, http://www.hackgolf.org/hackathons/golf/orientation.

27 Pennington, "In a Hole, Golf Considers Digging a Wider One."

Chapter 5

1 MacKenzie, *The Spirit of St. Andrews*, 61–2.

2 "DuPont Surlyn molding resins for golf ball manufacturing," DuPont, accessed July 29, 2013, http://www2.dupont.com/Surlyn/en_US/products/golfball_resins.html.

3 "Z-Star Golf Ball," accessed July 29, 2013, http://www.srixon.co.uk/golf-balls/z-star-pure-white/.

Chapter 6

1 Bob Cupp and Ron Whitten, *Golf's Grand Design: The Evolution of Golf Course Architecture in America* (CreateSpace, 2012), 75.

2 Josh Sens, "Pace of play problems? The Golden Bear blames the modern golf ball," *Golf*, July 29, 2013, accessed July 30, 2013, http://blogs.golf.com/presstent/2013/07/pace-of-play-problems-the-golden-bear-blames-the-modern-ball.html.

3 Moss, *The Kingdom of Golf in America*, 52–3.

4 MacKenzie, *The Spirit of St. Andrews*, 62.

5 MacKenzie, *The Spirit of St. Andrews*, 122.

6 MacKenzie, *The Spirit of St. Andrews*, 75.

7 Moss, *The Kingdom of Golf in America*, 284–5.

8 John McPhee, "The Orange Trapper," *The New Yorker* (July 1, 2013): 33.

9 Gary Wiren, *The PGA Manual of Golf* (New York: Macmillan, 1991), 242.

10 Neil Geoghegan, "U.S. Open Notes: Trevino, Graham talk up Merion," Daily Local News, accessed June 30, 2013, http://www.dailylocal.com/article/DL/20130611/SPORTS03/130619891.

11 Doak, *The Anatomy of a Golf Course*, 216.

12 Jack Nicklaus, *Golf My Way* (New York: Fireside, 1997), 316.

13 Nicklaus, *Golf My Way*, 317–18.

14 Doak, *The Anatomy of a Golf Course*, 20–2.

15 Doak, *The Anatomy of a Golf Course*, 24–5.

Chapter 7

1   John Cutler, ed., *Reports of Patent, Design, Trade Mark, and Other Cases* XXII (London: Great Britain Patent Office, 1905), 496.

2   MacKenzie, *The Spirit of St. Andrews*, 4.

Chapter 8

1   "Nitro Leisure Products v. Acushnet Company," FindLaw, accessed February 20, 2014, http://caselaw.findlaw.com/us-federal-circuit/1410780.html.

2   "Nitro Leisure Products v. Acushnet Company."

3   "Nitro Leisure Products v. Acushnet Company."

4   "Kasco 2013 Spring–Summer," accessed July 30, 2013, http://www.kasco.co.jp.

Chapter 9

1   "Tour ball markings," Golf WRX, accessed March 20, 2014, http://www.golfwrx.com/forums/topic/73162-tour-ball-markings/.

2   "Tour ball markings."

3   Murphy, *Golf in the Kingdom*, 100–1.

4   William Gibson, *Pattern Recognition, 2003* (New York: Berkley, 2005), 69.

5 *Goldfinger*, directed by Guy Hamilton (United Artists, 1964).

6 Karl Marx, *Capital*, Vol. I, in *Collected Works*, Vol. 35, trans. Samuel Moore and Edward Aveling (New York: International Publishers, 1996), 83.

7 "Titleist Pro V1."

Chapter 10

1 Bart Pfankuch, "Death by golf balls not all that uncommon," *Herald-Tribune*, accessed March 20, 2014, http://golf.heraldtribune.com/2010/11/29/death-by-golf-ball-not-all-that-uncommon/.

2 R. Michael Bomberger, "Golf Course Accidents: Injuries from Golf Balls, Golf Clubs, and Golf Carts," accessed March 27, 2014, http://www.avvo.com/legal-guides/ugc/golf-course-accidents-injuries-from-golf-balls-golf-clubs-and-golf-carts.

3 Brian H. Kaye, *Golf Balls, Boomerangs, and Asteroids* (Weinheim, Germany: Verlagsgesellschaft, 1996), 3.

4 Kaye, *Golf Balls, Boomerangs, and Asteroids*, 4.

Chapter 11

1 Murphy, *Golf in the Kingdom*, 27.

2 Ben Hogan, *Five Lessons: The Fundamentals of Modern Golf* (New York: Cornerstone, 1957), 84.

3 Murphy, *Golf in the Kingdom*, 29.

4 Murphy, *Golf in the Kingdom*, 85.

Chapter 12

1 Jones, *Golf Is My Game*, xvii.

2 Jones, *Golf Is My Game*, 72.

3 Hogan, *Five Lessons*, 37.

4 Hogan, *Five Lessons*, 18–19.

5 Jones, *Golf Is My Game*, 27.

6 Jones, *Golf Is My Game*, 28.

7 Jones, *Golf Is My Game*, 42.

8 Hogan, *Five Lessons*, 14.

9 Hogan, *Five Lessons*, 35.

10 Jones, *Golf Is My Game*, 28.

11 Nicklaus, *Golf My Way*, 17.

12 Nicklaus, *Golf My Way*, 16.

13 Nicklaus, *Golf My Way*, 15.

14 Nicklaus, *Golf My Way*, 18.

15 Nicklaus, *Golf My Way*, 18.

16 Nicklaus, *Golf My Way*, 18.

17 Jones, *Golf Is My Game*, 28.

18 Csikszentmihalyi, *Flow*, 61.

19 Jones, *Golf Is My Game*, 26.

20 Jones, *Golf Is My Game*, 27–8.

21 Hogan, *Five Lessons*, 15.

22 Nicklaus, *Golf My Way*, 22.

Chapter 13

1 Harvey Penick, *Harvey Penick's Little Red Book* (Norwalk, CT: Easton, 1992), 80.

2 Penick, *Harvey Penick's Little Red Book*, 90.

3 Joseph Parent, *Zen Golf: Mastering the Mental Game* (New York: Doubleday, 2002), xvii.

4 Parent, *Zen Golf*, 15.

5 Parent, *Zen Golf*, 35.

6 Parent, *Zen Golf*, 37.

7 Parent, *Zen Golf*, 44.

8 Murphy, *Golf in the Kingdom*, 16.

9 Murphy, *Golf in the Kingdom*, 63.

10 Murphy, *Golf in the Kingdom*, 168.

11 Murphy, *Golf in the Kingdom*, 169, 180.

Chapter 14

1 Murphy, *Golf in the Kingdom*, 26–7.

2 Murphy, *Golf in the Kingdom*, 28.

3 Murphy, *Golf in the Kingdom*, 32.

4 Murphy, *Golf in the Kingdom*, 170.

5 Parent, *Zen Golf*, 103–4.

6 Parent, *Zen Golf*, 153.

7 Murphy, *Golf in the Kingdom*, 32.

8 Murphy, *Golf in the Kingdom*, 17.

9 Murphy, *Golf in the Kingdom*, 129.

10 Herman Melville, *Moby-Dick, 1851* (New York: Norton, 1967), 168–9.

11 Murphy, *Golf in the Kingdom*, 176.

12 Murphy, *Golf in the Kingdom*, 102.

Chapter 15

1 Browning, *A History of Golf*, 60.

2 Browning, *A History of Golf*, 62–3.

3 Browning, *A History of Golf*, 19.

4 Browning, *A History of Golf*, 7.

5 Colt, MacKenzie, and Tillinghast, *Methods*, 42.

6 Colt, MacKenzie, and Tillinghast, *Methods*, 14–15.

7 MacKenzie, *The Spirit of St. Andrews*, 43.

8 Murphy, *Golf in the Kingdom*, 62–3.

9 Murphy, *Golf in the Kingdom*, 127–8.

10 Murphy, *Golf in the Kingdom*, 51–3.

11 Cupp and Whitten, *Golf's Grand Design*, 45.

12 Murphy, *Golf in the Kingdom*, 52.

Chapter 16

1 "Apollo 14 Lunar Surface Journal," National Aeronautics and Space Administration, accessed January 31, 2014, http://www.history.nasa.gov/alsj/a14/a14.clsout2.html.

2 Murphy, *Golf in the Kingdom*, 129–30.

3 Murphy, *Golf in the Kingdom*, 136.

Chapter 17

1 Darren Rovell, "Golf ball diving is big business," EPSN, accessed March 12, 2014, http://sports.espn.go.com/golf/playerschamp06/columns/story?id=2380969.

2 Bill Pennington, "The Burden and Boon of Lost Golf Balls," *On Par: The New York Times Golf Blog*, accessed July 24, 2013, http://onpar.blogs.nytimes.com/2010/05/02/the-burden-and-boon-of-lost-golf-balls/?_r=0.

3 McPhee, "The Orange Trapper," 31.

4 John Updike, Foreword to *Lost Balls: Great Holes, Tough Shots, and Bad Lies*, by Charles Lindsay (New York: Bullfinch, 2005).

5 Charles Lindsay, *Lost Balls: Great Holes, Tough Shots, and Bad Lies* (New York: Bullfinch, 2005).

6 Updike, Foreword.

7 Lindsay, *Lost Balls*.

8 McPhee, "The Orange Trapper," 30.

Chapter 18

1 Updike, Foreword.

2 Lindsay, *Lost Balls*.

3 Rovell, "Golf ball diving is big business."

4 Eliot, *The Rock*, 85.

5 Hugh Kenner, *Historical Fictions* (San Francisco: North Point Press, 1990), 86.

6 Christina Macfarlane, "Golf balls: 'Humanity's signature litter,'" CNN, accessed July 24, 2013, http://www.cnn.com/2009/SPORT/11/04/littering.golf.balls/.

7 McPhee, "The Orange Trapper," 31.

8 Saito, "Measuring the Lifecycle Carbon Footprint."

9 Macfarlane, "Golf balls: 'Humanity's signature litter.'"

10 Alan Weisman, *The World Without Us* (New York: Picador, 2007), 157.

11 Weisman, *The World Without Us*, 157.

12 Weisman, *The World Without Us*, 161.

13 Morton, *Hyperobjects*, 115.

INDEX